MAKING A DIFFERENCE

TEACHER'S TOOLKIT SERIES

I

Teaching for Success:
Developing Your Teacher Identity in Today's Classroom
Brad Olsen (UC–Santa Cruz)

2

Teaching English Learners:
Fostering Language and the Democratic Experience
Kip Téllez (UC–Santa Cruz)

3

Teaching Without Bells: What We Can Learn
from Powerful Practice in Small Schools
Joey Feldman (New Haven Unified School District)

4

Leading from the Inside Out:
Expanded Roles for Teachers in Equitable Schools
W. Norton Grubb and Lynda Tredway
(UC–Berkeley)

5

Teaching Toward Democracy:
Educators as Agents of Change
William Ayers (U of Ill–Chicago), Kevin Kumashiro (U of Ill–Chicago),
Erica Meiners (Northeastern Illinois University),
Therese Quinn (The Art Institute of Chicago), and David Stovall (U of Ill–Chicago)

6

Making a Difference:
Developing Meaningful Careers in Education
Karen Hunter Quartz (UCLA), Brad Olsen (UC–Santa Cruz),
Lauren Anderson (UCLA), and Kimberly Barraza Lyons (UCLA)

MAKING A DIFFERENCE

Developing Meaningful Careers in Education

Karen Hunter Quartz, Brad Olsen,
Lauren Anderson, and Kimberly Barraza Lyons

TEACHER'S TOOLKIT SERIES

Paradigm Publishers

Boulder • London

Copyright © 2010 Paradigm Publishers

Published in the United States by Paradigm Publishers,
2845 Wilderness Place, Suite 200, Boulder, CO 80301 USA.
Paradigm Publishers is the trade name of Birkenkamp
& Company, LLC,
Dean Birkenkamp, President and Publisher.

Library of Congress Cataloging-in-Publication Data

Making a difference : developing meaningful careers in
    education / Karen Hunter Quartz . . . [et al].
        p. cm. — (Teacher's toolkit series)
    Includes bibliographical references and index.
    ISBN 978-1-59451-708-2 (pbk : alk. paper)
    1. Teaching—Vocational guidance—United States.
    2. Effective teaching—United States.   3. Teachers—
    Training of—United States. I. Quartz, Karen Hunter,
    1963–
    LB1775.2.M35   2009
    370.23—dc22

                                          2009017112

Printed and bound in the United States of America on
acid-free paper that meets the standards of the American
National Standard for Permanence of Paper for Printed
Library Materials.

Design and composition by Cindy Young.

14 13 12 11 10   1 2 3 4 5

CONTENTS

SERIES FOREWORD

T HIS TEACHER'S TOOLKIT series is a set of six related books written for prospective, new, and experienced teachers who are committed to students and families, who conceive of themselves as agents of democratic change, and who are eager to think more deeply, more broadly, and more practically about their work in education. All six books succinctly link theory with practice, present extended arguments for improving education, and wrap their discussions around successful examples of the topics in question.

Although each book is its own resource, the books in the Toolkit series share some common views about teaching. For one, all of the books treat teachers not as mere deliverers of curriculum but as active, three-dimensional professionals capable of diagnosing student learning, developing powerful educational experiences, assessing and adjusting student learning, and forming productive relationships with children and adults in schools. Another view all of the books share is that teaching is hard work that is among the most important kinds of work any society requires. My grandmother used to say that no society can survive without farmers or teachers. I think that is still true. Teaching is undeniably difficult work, but it is also frequently enjoyable work because it is so challenging, meaningful, and success oriented. These books are for teachers who have accepted the challenges of teaching because they relish the satisfaction of the work, they enjoy helping young people grow, and they know that quality education is necessary for the health of our world.

A third commonality about teaching among these books is their shared presumption that teachers are always looking for ways to improve. Teaching is a profession in which one enters as a novice, develops expertise over time, and continues to grow and change throughout the whole of one's career. The Toolkit books are written for teachers at multiple points in their career cycle: Beginning teachers will learn new ways to think about learning, students, and about what it means to become a successful educator. Early- and middle-career teachers can reflect on their own practice in light of the ideas, strategies, and stories of these books—and they can use the books to deepen and broaden their future work. Veteran teachers can see themselves and their varied experiences inside the perspectives of the books, as well as figure out how they can continue to challenge themselves and their students—and perhaps take on other kinds of education work such as mentoring newer teachers, advocating for students on a broader stage, or writing about their own teaching. No matter where readers are in their education careers, these books offer powerful learning and useful opportunities for professional reflection.

The six books are sequenced to loosely follow both the career cycle of teaching and the fact that, as teachers progress, they often widen their sphere of influence. Book 1 in the series is *Teaching for Success: Developing Your Teacher Identity in Today's Classroom*, by Brad Olsen. This book focuses on the processes of "becoming a teacher" and explores how to teach well in this contemporary age. Wrapping its conversations about teacher development around the core concept of teacher identity, the book offers its own teacher learning experience: how to recognize, adjust, and maximize the many ways your personal self and your professional self become integrated in your teaching work.

Book 2, *Teaching English Learners: Fostering Language and the Democratic Experience*, by Kip Téllez, focuses on what teachers can do in their classrooms in order to better understand and more effectively teach English learners. Drawing from research and experience not only on learning and teaching but also on culture, language, immigration, and contemporary politics, Téllez offers a unique guide for use by U.S. teachers interested in deeply and compassionately supporting the growth of students whose native language is not English.

Book 3 in the series is *Teaching Without Bells: What We Can Learn from Powerful Instruction in Small Schools*, by Joey Feldman. This book offers a valuable look at how teaching and learning are fundamentally influenced by school size. The book's premise is that student and teacher experiences in education are direct functions of their school's size (and its accompanying influence on how schools are organized). Focusing on challenges and benefits of teaching in small high schools, Feldman's book helps readers consider where they might want to teach and—no matter the size of their school site—how they can teach well by maximizing lessons from the small schools movement.

Book 4, *Leading from the Inside Out: Expanded Roles for Teachers in Equitable Schools*, by Norton Grubb and Lynda Tredway, opens up the professional world of the teacher by offering new ways to think about school reform from the vantage point of the teacher. The authors make a compelling case for teachers as the key ingredient in education reform and schools as the lever for democratic educational change. Presenting a blueprint for a new kind of school in which teachers are not only classroom instructors but education reformers as well, Grubb and Tredway illustrate why we have the schools we have today and how broad-minded teachers can transform them into successful schools for tomorrow.

Book 5, *Teaching Toward Democracy: Educators as Agents of Change*, by William Ayers, Kevin Kumashiro, Erica Meiners, Therese Quinn, and David Stovall, also considers teachers as agents of change on a broader scale. The authors share their ideas about how teachers can better humanize schooling for students, combat some of the current failings of market models of education, and extend their teaching work past the school day and outside the school walls. Their book invites readers into a view of education through the eyes of students, and it provides thoughtful strategies to enact teaching for social justice as not just a popular slogan but an authentic focus on human rights and social equity for all.

And, to close out the series, Book 6, *Making a Difference: Developing Meaningful Careers in Education*, by Karen Hunter Quartz, Brad Olsen, Lauren Anderson, and Kimberly Barraza Lyons, looks at whole careers in education. This book examines the dynamic lives and work of several educators in Los Angeles and investigates why teachers stay in the classroom or shift to other kinds of education roles, such as school administrator, curriculum coordinator, or teacher mentor. The book unpacks the sometimes maddening complexity of the teaching profession and offers a roadmap for how teachers can, themselves, re-main challenged and satisfied as educators without relaxing their com-mitments to students.

There are different approaches to reading the books in this series. One way is to consider the whole series as a coherent set of sequenced conversations about teaching. In this manner, you might read the books one at a time, all the way through, inserting yourself into the text of the books: Do the stories and experiences in the books ring true for you? How will you use these books to improve your practice, broaden your influence, and deepen your professional satisfaction? You might imagine, as you read the books this way, that you are sitting in a room with the authors—listening to their ideas, questioning them, ac-tively engaging with their arguments, or talking back to the text when necessary.

Or perhaps you might use these books as textbooks—as thoughtful primers on selected topics that interest you. In this manner, you might pick and choose particular chapters to study: Which specific ideas will you implement in your teaching tomorrow? Are there further readings or key resources that you will hunt down and look at on your own? What concrete activities will you try out? Write notes in the margins of the books and return to the chapters regularly. Photocopy single pages (not whole chapters, please!) to share with peers. Use the books as you plan lessons or design curricula. Engage with the reflection questions at the end of each book's chapters. You will find occasionally in the mar-gins cross-references on specific topics to other books in the series. When you read "Cross-Reference, See Book 2 …" you can use the numbered list of titles on p. ii to correlate each reference to the in-tended book.

Or, you may pick some of the books to read collectively with other educators—maybe with your teacher education cohort, or as a group of teachers working with a mentor, or perhaps as part of a teacher inquiry group that you set up with colleagues. Group discussion of these books allows their arguments, perspectives, and examples to prompt your own collective reflection and professional growth: What themes from the books call out to you? What points might you disagree with? How might different educators among you interpret parts of these books in different, perhaps competing, ways? How can these books inspire you to create specific collaborative projects or teacher networks at your school site? You may find the reflection questions at the end of each chapter particularly useful for group conversation.

This series of books is called the "Teacher's Toolkit," but maybe, for some, the idea of a *toolkit* for teachers may not, at first glance, be apt. Picturing a toolkit could conjure images of a steel toolbox or superhero belt full of hardware for educators—a diagnostic screwdriver, the clawhammer of homework, a set of precision wrenches for adjusting student learning on the fly. Such images are, well, just too instrumental. They risk suggesting that teaching is mechanical or automatic, or that what good educators do is select utensils from their box to apply when needed. That doesn't describe the kind of teaching I know and love. It erroneously suggests that students are to be fastened with bolts or hammered into obedience, or that learning is gut-wrenchingly rigid. And, to my mind, such a view treats teachers as technicians trained by rote, using tools given to them by others, following directions written on the outside of the box.

Instead, the authors of these books conceive of education as less fixed, more fluid, less finished, more uncertain, and certainly far more complicated than anything for which traditional tools would work. These authors—based on their own years of experience as classroom teachers, educational researchers, school administrators, and university professors—view education similarly to educational philosopher John Dewey when, in 1934, he wrote:

> About 40 years ago, a new idea dawned in education. Educators began to see that education should parallel life, that the school should reproduce the child's world. In this new type of education the child, instead of the curriculum, became the centre of interest, and since the child is active, changing, creative—education ceased to be static, [and] became dynamic and creative in response to the needs of the child.[1]

Like Dewey, I understand teaching and learning to be context-specific, highly creative, dynamically student-centered activities that are as complicated and multifaceted as life itself. And just as important.

So let's reimagine the analogy of a teacher's toolkit. A *toolkit* for teachers could instead be a metaphor for a thoughtful, useful, provocative bundle of perspectives, theories, and approaches for teachers—a set of lively teaching discussions written by different authors who share some common ground. This bundle would empathize with teachers since its authors are all teachers, as well as education researchers and writers: they know both how difficult and how rewarding teaching can be. But it would also exhort teachers not to fall down on the job—not to shirk their work, make excuses, or lessen their resolve to support students.

The bundle of teaching conversations could share stories from the classroom that reveal teaching to be kaleidoscopic: made up of thousands of shifting views, hundreds of competing relations, and dozens of different ways to succeed with children. The stories would reveal how to be a great teacher and why doing so is so damned important. The bundle of ideas and perspectives would include actual examples of good teaching, lesson ideas, and lots of research tidbits useful for prospective and practicing educators. Yes, that could be a toolkit I would want to own. It would be a kit full of thoughtful perspectives, research summaries, wisdom of practice, and impassioned words of advice from handpicked educationalists. An "idea kit," really. A boxed set of thoughtful primers on how to teach well for social change in the current global climate.

John Dewey famously built binaries in his writing—teaching is either this or that; students learn in this way but not in that way—only to collapse the binary in the end and suggest that education is too complicated for easy contradictions. So I'll take a page from Dewey's playbook and attempt the same. Maybe we can consider this book series as not an either/or. Not as *either* a box of teaching instruments *or* a collection of thoughtful conversations about education, but as both: a set of tangible strategies for teachers to make their own and a loosely bundled collection of professional arguments for use by educators in order to think for themselves, but in deeper and newer ways than before. That's the way that I prefer to envision this teacher's toolkit.

No matter how you choose to make use of the books in the Teacher's Toolkit, it is our sincere hope that you will find value in them. We have tried to make them accessible, conversational, substantive, and succinct. We all believe that teaching is a fundamentally important profession, and, if this world is to improve and grow, it will be because our teachers can help future generations to become wise, creative, and critical thinkers who put their ideas into action toward improving the societies they will inherit. You are an essential part of that human process.

—Brad Olsen
University of California, Santa Cruz

NOTE

1. Dewey, J. 1934. "Tomorrow May Be too Late: Save the Schools Now." Reprinted in J. Boydston (ed.) 1986 *John Dewey: The Later Works, 1925–1953: 1933–1934, Vol. 9.* Carbondale, I: Southern Illinois University Press. 386.

ACKNOWLEDGMENTS

THE RESEARCH REPORTED in this book was made possible by the generous support of the Stuart Foundation. For five years, the foundation supported UCLA's Urban Teacher Education Collaborative—an ambitious set of activities to deepen, extend, and study the reach of Center X's Teacher Education Program. As part of this collaborative, we were privileged to study the retention and careers of more than a thousand Center X graduates, seven of whom we portray here in depth. Although their real names are not included, we extend our greatest thanks to the committed educators we called Armando, Barbara, Christine, Diana, Emma, Frances, and Grace. Your work has inspired us, and we hope that many others learn from your creative career paths.

We also wish to thank our colleagues who participated in the larger longitudinal research study: Katherine Masyn, Andrew Thomas, Joanna Goode, and Eileen Lai Horng. Our lively research meetings and your many contributions helped make this book a reality. We were also fortunate to have the expert counsel and advice of several researchers throughout our study, in particular, Jeannie Oakes, Richard Ingersoll, Linda Darling-Hammond, Barnett Berry, and Marilyn Cochran-Smith. Finally, we would like to thank our Center X colleagues who work tirelessly each day to prepare teachers to transform public schooling in Los Angeles, especially Jody Priselac, Nancy Parachini, Megan Loef Franke, John Rogers, and Eloise Lopez Metcalfe.

INTRODUCTION

The core of my work is teaching—helping students learn—yet the conditions of my work make teaching difficult and often perpetuate inequity and problematic school practices. How do I advance the core work of teaching and learning while also working to change schools, especially for students who have been traditionally underserved by public education? What is the best way for me to make a difference? And how do I do this in a way that allows me to lead a happy and balanced life?

IKE ALL GOOD PUZZLES, this one has no easy answer. There is no one best way to make a difference or lead a happy life. Nor is there one best way to fix schools, retain good teachers, or leave no child behind. Complex issues demand complex responses. But just as understanding the complexity inherent in this career puzzle is key, so is the ability to take action and construct careers in education that make sense within the context of our lives. What seems like an appropriate career pathway to some will seem wrongheaded to others. Moreover, our culture and media tend to oversimplify the choices that educators face. This book dispels the myth of a simple career choice dichotomy—to stay in or leave classroom teaching—by representing the range of

This book dispels the myth of a simple career choice dichotomy—to stay in or leave classroom teaching.

responses and career pathways that enable educators to make a difference. This range of pathways is based on data from hundreds of change-minded educators, seven of whom we portray in detail.

Diana has been teaching kindergarten in the same classroom for a decade and has no plans to leave. Emma, too, has worked at the same school—as a teacher and instructional leader—for the past ten years. She is committed to education but is considering roles that could pull her away from the classroom. Armando originally aspired to be a civil rights lawyer, before turning to teaching to make more of a difference. He was then quickly invited out of the classroom to become an administrator, but now he is not sure he should have left so soon. After six years in the classroom, Barbara began a gradual move into school leadership, where she intends to be a strong voice on issues of policy and practice. Christine worked in three different schools, including a start-up charter, and then left for graduate school because she became frustrated by the conditions of urban schools. Once she has developed a more systemic perspective, she hopes to return to the public education system in a way that improves learning opportunities for adolescents at risk of dropping out. After teaching for four years, Grace was offered a district position leading new teacher support programs and other district initiatives. Since then, she has scaled that work back to 40 percent time and taken on another part-time job as an assistant principal at a local elementary school. Though earlier efforts to create a new high school were stymied, Grace is still interested in the possibility of helping to develop and lead a small progressive public school. Frances, a middle school math teacher, has been a vocal advocate of teacher professionalism during her nine years in the classroom. She has served as a content expert and teacher leader, and she plans to continue to expand this work in the future while also staying in classroom teaching. These are seven of the nation's six million teachers. Each has a unique career story, and each is struggling to make a difference amid the current conditions that define public education.

From 2000 to 2007 we studied the career pathways of Diana, Emma, Armando, Barbara, Christine, Grace, Frances, and more than a thousand other educators in their first through tenth years in the profession. *In this book we share their stories and insights against a backdrop that maps out the complexities inherent in the career decisions they all face. These complexities include the hierarchical nature of the educational system; the history of teaching as a gendered, low-status profession; inadequate school resources and funding; the day-to-day conditions of schools as workplaces; and many other factors.* Taken together, these complex factors portray "making a difference" as a daunting prospect. Layering on the complexities of everyday life—maturation, parenting and caretaking, paying bills, and so on—can make this quest even more overwhelming.

Focus point

It is perhaps not surprising that almost half of the nation's teachers leave the classroom after five years of service. In our most high-poverty urban schools, attrition is even higher, with about a fifth of the teaching faculty turning over every single year. For this reason, policymakers and the press have sounded the alarm: schools must figure out a way to keep their teachers. Too often, however, the response is an appeal to recruit and retain teachers that can weather the storm that defines teachers' work, especially in urban schools plagued by dismal conditions. As a culture, we often portray these recruits as heroes—courageously fighting against all odds for the interests of young people dealt a raw hand. As stirring and inspiring as these heroic images are, they rarely capture the reality of constructing and sustaining meaningful careers in urban education.

Consider the career development of Jaime Escalante, whose story is told in the movie *Stand and Deliver*.[1] Renowned for introducing Advanced Placement calculus to high-poverty youth in East Los Angeles's Garfield

High School, Escalante was clearly driven by a belief in the capacity of students to work hard and master challenging mathematical knowledge and skills—mastery that would open doors to a better future. Escalante believed fervently in the power of education for social change. As he famously warned students, "The day you quit school, you condemn yourself to a future of poverty." But Jaime Escalante did not work alone. Over ten years, he helped to groom a whole cadre of teachers to increase the rigor of feeder math courses to ensure that students would be prepared for the challenge of calculus. He also had an outstanding principal, Henry Gradillas, who bent and changed many rules to enable Escalante and his colleagues to develop their math program with sufficient professional freedom and responsibility. Though the movie portrayed Escalante as a lone hero, the truth is that he was part of a network of committed educators and his work (and freedom to teach as he wanted) took hold at and grew during a fertile moment in the school's history.

As the Garfield High math program expanded in size and acclaim following the movie's release, several factors combined to lead to the program's eventual demise and Escalante's move to another school. Gradillas, the maverick principal, was reassigned. Class sizes soared, some to more than fifty students. In addition, the singular focus and spotlight on Escalante, as an individual hardworking teacher, led to friction among colleagues. At the same time, Escalante's success sparked broader debate and controversy; Escalante received threats and hate mail and eventually was denied his post as math department chair. In 1991, he moved to a school in Sacramento to restart his program. After making some progress in the new school, Escalante, then in his sixties, became the host of *Futures*, an acclaimed PBS series on math- and science-based careers. In 1998, he retired to his native Bolivia to teach part time at a local university and in his home studio.

Although he is widely revered as an educational hero, Jaime Escalante and his career in urban education illustrate themes we found in our own research; enacting your core commitments to social change through education requires enormous creativity, fortitude, and perseverance, but it also demands sufficient professional autonomy and supportive social networks. Escalante's principal supported his work, and a group of colleagues helped make that work happen within an urban high school context that is typically hostile to structural change. Without supportive relationships and professional autonomy, it is likely that Escalante may never have achieved the success he found. He may have acted on the impulse he felt his first day at Garfield and left the classroom for his old job at a computer factory. Escalante's story helps us introduce the stories of teachers in our study because it reminds us that many of the myths perpetuated about teaching—as heroic, challenging, solitary, single-minded work—obscure the complex realities. In reality, educators' hard work often reflects far more variation, involves as many frustrations as successes, is mediated by multiple people and factors, and is frequently misrepresented in public discourse and popular culture.

The interplay of these multiple factors and their influence on teachers' career paths is the primary focus of this book. As was true for Jaime Escalante, careers in education are guided by a variety of pushes and pulls, satisfactions and frustrations, hopes and doubts, personal demands and professional rewards. Yet the common view, as reflected in sensational headlines about teacher attrition, is that you decide every spring between teaching and leaving the classroom. To stay or to leave. In addition to being overly simplistic, this dichotomy fails to recognize the changing nature of work and careers both inside and outside education. Today's generation of workers can expect to change jobs, careers even, five to seven times during their lives. A career in education is no exception: for many educators, it now constitutes several phases or stages, often encompassing different roles within the field and leaving a multifaceted, unique, and sometimes even zigzagging trail in its wake.

In Chapter 1, based on extensive longitudinal data, we map out this increasingly complex and fluid career landscape and describe many educators' struggle with an essential tension: *How do I stay connected to the core work of teaching—directly facilitating student learning—in a profession that rewards me for taking on roles and responsibilities beyond the classroom?* This tension shapes what it means to make a difference in education and leads some teachers to ask whether making a difference is most powerfully framed in terms of direct work with students, or broader efforts toward structural changes that promise benefits for all students or groups of students. The educators we profile in this book attempt to reconcile this tension by embracing both frames. Moreover, they conceive of their impact (or the difference they make) across many dimensions—student learning, school-level change, parent education, district and state policy, community activism, teacher development, and so on. As change-minded educators, their careers twist and turn in ways that attend to these many dimensions. For them, making a difference means working within a system and trying to change it at the same time.

Focus point

Making a difference means working within a system and trying to change it at the same time.

We expect this book to be of most interest to change-minded educators contemplating their own careers. So throughout the chapters, we directly address educators—often posing questions for reflection and possible career pathways for consideration. That said, we also hope that researchers and policymakers working to study and improve the profession of education will find this book useful. For this reason, we have included as an appendix a list of related publications that share findings from our larger, longitudinal research project.

All the teachers you will meet in this book have taught in challenging urban contexts. They have all exercised their professional autonomy and responsibility to serve students well. They have all navigated social networks of educators, friends, and family who buoy or dampen their reform spirit. And, as change-minded educators, they have all committed to a common set of values and a shared goal to change society through schooling. The core chapters of this book—Chapters 2, 3, and 4—tell their stories in terms of three commonalities: exercising professional autonomy, building social networks, and making a difference. Each chapter begins with a conceptual frame that outlines how the history, structures, and culture of schooling define what it means to be a professional, embedded in social networks, and working for change. Conceptual frames then lead into the stories of our seven educators. In Chapter 2, the stories of Armando, Barbara, Christine, and Diana speak directly to the issues of autonomy and freedom. Chapter 3 tells the stories of Emma, Frances, and Grace as examples of educators who have built powerful social networks that define their school-based, professional, and personal relationships. Chapter 4 revisits all seven stories, weaving them together to examine how teachers themselves make sense of what it means to "make a difference." Throughout these chapters we offer sidebars for readers interested in learning more about policy contexts and possible roles in education.

Our analysis culminates in a final chapter entitled "The Dream Job." Drawing on the voices of educators, we argue that this "dream job" is an ideal, rather than a particular role, title, or workplace. In short, a "dream job" is one that allows educators sufficient professional autonomy, embeds them in a variety of supportive social networks, and enables them to make a difference across many dimensions of the educational system—all while living happy and balanced lives. Based on our analysis of the history and culture of teaching as well as the educational workforce, we speculate about what it will take to create conditions, roles, and structures that might approach this ideal. We close with the voices of our seven educators and their hopes for the future.

NOTE

1. Jesse Jessness, "Stand and Deliver Revisited," *Reason,* July 2002; http://www.reason.com/news/show/28479.html; http://www.thefutureschannel.com/jaime_escalante/jaime_escalante_bio.php.

CHAPTER ONE

THE LANDSCAPE OF CAREERS IN EDUCATION

ACH FALL, the University of California at Los Angeles's (UCLA) Teacher Education Program welcomes 170 new novice teachers—each eager to join the education profession. From 2001 to 2004, we surveyed 383 incoming students and asked about their career plans. Three-quarters of these new recruits said they expected their professional role to extend beyond the classroom. One-fifth did not even expect to be in the classroom within five years of graduating from the program. What they expected to be doing, however, was far from clear for most of them. Despite their uncertainty, there was a high degree of consensus among this group that whatever they did, wherever they went, their work and actions would make a difference in the world. Some talked of becoming principals, some of starting schools, some of running for office. Most, however, seemed to have only a vague or tentative plan for their futures—one that started with teaching.

Planning for the future is, of course, wrought with uncertainty. Where life takes any of us, and why, is a process that depends on our own individual efficacy and our own decisions, but also on factors and circumstances beyond

There are "myriad institutional forces that shape you into something else."

our control. As one teacher put it, there are "myriad institutional forces that shape you into something else." These forces push and pull us in different ways—some apparent, some hidden from view. Salary schedules, for example, often guide career decisions because money is a powerful and highly visible marker of social value in our culture. Educators are often lured out of the classroom because of the corresponding boost in status and monetary reward. Other forces are more subtle, like the commonly held view that high-achieving or ambitious individuals are "too smart" or "too talented" to be teachers for long. Few say this out loud, but our research revealed how this tradition of teaching as low-status work affected the career decisions of many teachers, some of whom were cherry-picked out of the classroom for seemingly "more important" or "more intellectual" work. We also heard many stories of teachers who fought hard against this expectation and proudly stayed rooted in the classroom. By sharing teachers' experiences with the pushes and pulls of the education profession, we hope that readers will be able to make sense of their own careers and purposely steer themselves in fulfilling directions.

This chapter sets the stage for the book's core chapters—2, 3, and 4—where we share the stories of seven educators and their career development, specifically their struggles to exercise professional autonomy, build supportive social networks, and make a difference. These seven stories are part of our larger study of more than a thousand educators in their first through tenth year of the profession. To understand the context of these careers, we first contrast two teaching traditions to characterize and distinguish the change-minded identity shared among the educators we studied. Second, we provide a brief overview of our longitudinal data in order to map out the vast array of opportunities and career pathways available to these change-minded educators. This data leads to a discussion of the changing nature of the educational workforce and the next generation of teachers. We close the chapter with a brief overview of the literature on career cycles in order to also recognize the powerful role that time, maturation, and life circumstances play in career development.

TEACHING TRADITIONS

Like most professions, teaching has a strong tradition that in large part defines its social value and significance. Rarely, however, is this tradition of teaching associated with powerful political or intellectual work. Put simply, teaching is not considered a high-status occupation in the United States. The reasons for this are many and varied. Teaching has long been a solid middle-class job with a union behind it that has historically affiliated more with manufacturing and labor unions than professional associations (Murphy 1990). Its salary structure, being front-loaded and mostly horizontal (meaning that a twenty-year veteran teacher does not make significantly more than a first-year beginner), is at odds with many other professions that offer rapidly increasing levels of status, pay, and autonomy (Lortie 1975). Lack of respect for teaching has a long and well-documented history in the United States and many other countries. This history recounts the feminization of the teaching workforce, its link to childcare, the commonsense notion that anyone can teach—and do so on a temporary basis—and the resultant low pay and low status (Apple 1985; Herbst 1989; Lortie 1975; Tyack 1974). Introduce yourself as a teacher at a party and you will likely experience the telltale smile that says, "Oh, how nice that you work with children," implying in many cases that working with children is less important, less intellectual, and less prestigious than working with adults.

In recent years, however, concerted efforts have been made to professionalize teaching and challenge the traditional conception that anyone can teach—that little specialized knowledge and preparation are required of

Cross-Reference

For a related discussion of society's perception of the teaching profession, see Book 1, Chapter 1.

teachers (Darling-Hammond and Bransford 2007; Darling-Hammond 1997, 2000; Shulman 1986). *Although many outside the profession continue to hold teaching in relatively low esteem, educators and education researchers have*

Focus point

increasingly turned toward conceptions of teaching as meaningful, difficult, professional work that deepens and grows over a decades-long tenure. This new tradition of viewing teaching as a challenging and distinguished profession is symbolized by efforts such as the National Board of Professional Teaching Standards and the many professional organizations that support advances in teaching and learning.

Most of the educators we studied align with this new tradition, yet with a twist. In addition to teaching professionals, they view themselves as social reformers or activists. Their motivations for entering the teaching profession stand in stark contrast to reasons traditionally cited for doing so. More than three decades ago, Lortie (1975) identified "material benefits" and "time compatibility" as frequently cited reasons for entering teaching. Many people still view teaching—long identified as "women's work"—as a career that allows them maximal flexibility to raise a family or pursue other interests, given that the work day ends early, and teachers' summers are typically free. When we surveyed novice teachers at UCLA's Teacher Education Program, however, we found that job security as well as the school calendar and hours were not at all the "potent recruitment resource" that Lortie once found. The relative lack of importance these novice educators placed on material benefits and time compatibility perhaps reflected their young age and idealism. However, a survey of educators with a few years of teaching under their belts revealed a similar trend.

For example, when asked why they stay in the profession of education, eight out of ten fifth-year educators surveyed responded that changing the world and furthering social justice were either extremely or very important reasons for staying in teaching; and 81 percent similarly responded that they stayed because they were attached to the kids and the community. About two-thirds of those teachers also cited a commitment to working in a low-income community as an extremely or very important reason for staying in education. In contrast, just over a third cited job security, and less than half cited the school calendar and work hours as extremely or very important reasons for staying.

Our interpretation of these reported reasons for teaching is that "changing the world and furthering social justice" provides for the teachers in our study a powerful alternative frame for defining one's social value and status. In contrast to the relative lack of monetary reward and the traditional conception of teaching as low-status work, change-minded educators rely on a different view. They connect themselves to a collective identity that offers an alternative reward system rooted in a long and noble history of education as the very foundation of our political system. As Thomas Jefferson argued more than two centuries ago, public schooling holds the key to our democracy, preparing citizens to be "guardians of their own liberty." Today, an increasing number of teachers identify themselves as change-minded educators and invoke this and other democratic aims of schooling. They seek to eradicate the inequitable conditions and outcomes of American education and view their work as influencing the broader social and political economy. These professionals appeal to the rich tradition of educators as powerful agents of change—in contrast with compliant women who care for and educate children to be dutiful citizens. This change-minded, equity-oriented, activist perspective is the one held by many of those who enter UCLA's Teacher Education Program, including the seven teachers profiled in the coming chapters.

These professionals appeal to the rich tradition of educators as powerful agents of change.

A VAST ARRAY OF OPPORTUNITIES

Let us turn now to the actual career pathways of the 1,084 educators we studied. All of these educators began their journey at UCLA in a social-justice–oriented, urban teacher education program. The program, an intensive two-year preservice program leading to state certification and a master's degree in education, works to specifically prepare its participants for careers in urban high-poverty schools (Oakes 1996; Olsen et al. 2005; Quartz and TEP Research Group 2003). Similar to the teacher workforce nationwide, the vast majority of graduates of UCLA's Teacher Education Program are women, but they are a younger and more ethnically diverse group than is generally seen in teacher education programs: only 35 percent are white, 25 percent are Hispanic, 6 percent are African American, and 32 percent are Asian. This demographic profile is significant given the growing "demographic divide" between increasingly diverse student populations and a still overwhelmingly white middle-class teaching force. Most of the program's teaching candidates are also graduates of selective undergraduate institutions, and many grew up in the same type of urban communities in which they seek to serve as educators. For the most part, these individuals entered teaching looking for a challenging career that would enable them to make a difference in the lives of children and the future of low-income communities. They sought out a career in teaching with an eye toward changing the world through education, and they entered UCLA's Teacher Education Program at least in part because of the social justice philosophy it espouses.

Each spring for six years, we sent surveys to these program graduates in order to track their career retention and movement. The surveys included information regarding the factors that keep teachers teaching and push and pull them away from the classroom—allowing for a deeper understanding of the motivations behind teachers' professional decisions. Additional surveys were also administered to participants just prior to entering and exiting UCLA's program, in order to better track the perceptions and intentions of teachers just starting preparation and employment as teachers. Data collected as part of this longitudinal study helps us paint a portrait of one population of well-prepared educators working in urban schools and provide a backdrop for the more detailed and nuanced accounts related in this book.

As part of this longitudinal study, graduates were asked annually to classify their professional role into one of seven categories: (1) full-time classroom teacher, (2) part-time classroom teacher, (3) substitute teacher, (4) administrator, (5) inside K–12 education in another role, (6) outside K–12 education in another role, or (7) left education entirely. Response information, along with analyses of survey data from teachers nationwide, indicates that graduates of UCLA's Teacher Education Program have higher classroom retention rates than do other beginning teachers. In other words, a greater percentage of UCLA teachers in their first five years away from the program maintain their roles as full-time classroom teachers than do other early career teachers, taken together as a group. Yet, when we compare these UCLA teachers to a comparable set of high-qualified and diverse early career teachers nationwide, most differences in retention disappear—signifying that retention may be importantly related to the quality of teacher preparation a candidate receives. What distinguishes the UCLA teachers the most is the schools in which they work—and the fact that many are staying over time in our nation's most challenging high-poverty urban schools. Where they go when they leave these urban classrooms and how they classify their professional roles is a story the longitudinal study helps to reveal.

All graduates of UCLA's Teacher Education Program started as classroom teachers in the high-poverty schools in and around Los Angeles; yet ten years later there is remarkable diversity in the career paths they have pursued. Data suggests that the vast majority of graduates have remained connected to the field of urban education, but that many have transitioned out of full-time classroom teaching. For the most part, rather than pursuing an unrelated career, these classroom leavers have shifted into other educational roles. *In fact, 70 percent of the graduates who leave the classroom have taken on other roles in the field of education, either within the K–12 school system or outside of it, rather than depart from education completely. Such roles include school principal, bilingual and induction coordinator, after-school program director, museum educator, educational software developer, and college professor. Despite leaving the classroom, these "teacher leavers" appear committed to education as a profession.* Moreover, many who have left the classroom at one point end up returning later in their careers.

Focus point

Most research on teachers' careers is cross-sectional. That is, it looks at a group, for example fifth-year teachers, and considers their career movement the following year in order to come up with a retention rate for, in this case, fifth-year teachers. What this method fails to do, however, is capture career movement over time—for example, before and after the fifth career year. In contrast, our longitudinal study looked at the *same group* of educators each year. Taking into account the difficulty of tracking the same individuals over time and the resulting missing data, we came up with the following career pathways chart of a representative subsample of 432 teachers for whom we have consistent role data.

As Figure 1.1 illustrates, there is an amazing diversity and range of career pathways in urban education—simply for the first eight years. This map of graduates' career movement over time shows the fifty-seven unique observed pathways—in addition to consistent full-time classroom teaching—that these 432 graduates followed. Whereas cross-sectional analyses can offer information about how many first-year teachers end up as teachers in their eighth year, longitudinal pathways also show the paths these teachers took between years one and eight— how many reported being full-time classroom teachers *every year* since having entered the profession, and how many reported having held other primary roles along the way. As Figure 1.1 shows, the consistent full-time classroom teaching pathway accounts for 95 percent of graduates in their third year but only 68 percent of graduates in their seventh year.[1] "Stayers" like these who remained in classroom teaching over their entire pathway represent 76 percent of the sample, and those who changed roles or left one or more times represented 24 percent of the sample. Of those 105 graduates, 59 percent changed roles/left once, 31 percent changed roles/left twice, and 10 percent changed roles/left three or four times. Considering that the average years in education for the sample is five, it is notable that 41 percent of these graduates changed roles two or more times. Of these 105 role changers/leavers, 84 (80 percent) changed roles at some point within the field of education. Additionally, although we see some pathways that involve leaving education, these should not be misunderstood as necessarily *ending* outside the profession. The chart shows that 105 of the 432 graduates with complete data changed roles at some point in their respective careers, with 34 of those 105 having left education at some point. Of those 34 leavers, nearly one-third returned to education as full-time classroom teachers (n=5), part-time teachers (n=1), and other roles in education outside of K–12 schooling (n=5). Graduate A, for example, moved in and out of the profession over the course of her first through seventh year working in education.

Our point in sharing this pathways chart is to dispel the myth that teachers either teach or leave. Rather, there are a variety of possible career pathways open to educators, and initial movement away from full-time classroom teaching is not necessarily permanent. We believe that the existence of "shifting" roles within urban education

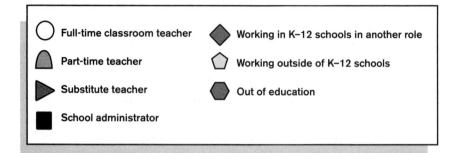

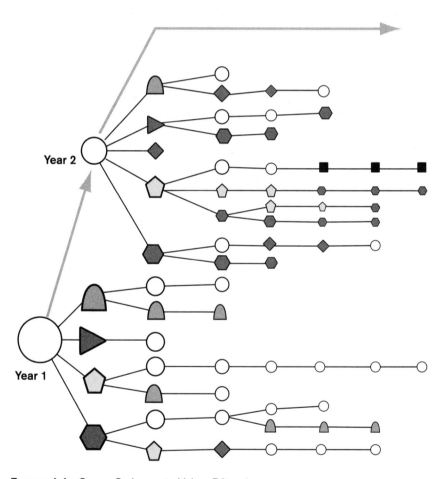

Figure 1.1. Career Pathways in Urban Education

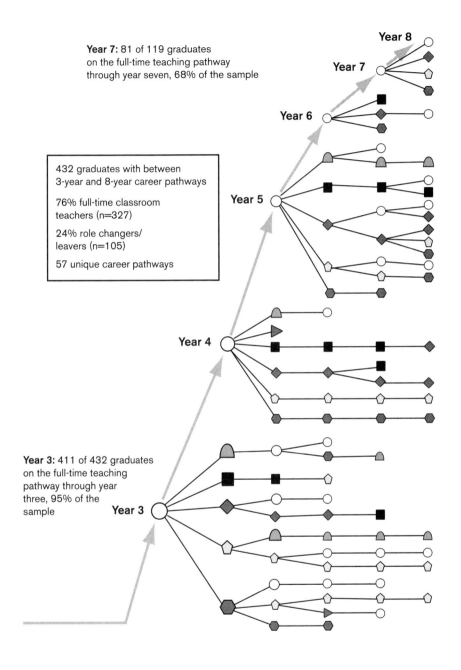

Year 8

Year 7: 81 of 119 graduates on the full-time teaching pathway through year seven, 68% of the sample

Year 7

Year 6

432 graduates with between 3-year and 8-year career pathways

76% full-time classroom teachers (n=327)

24% role changers/ leavers (n=105)

57 unique career pathways

Year 5

Year 4

Year 3: 411 of 432 graduates on the full-time teaching pathway through year three, 95% of the sample

Year 3

warrants careful consideration and a career frame that does not automatically bemoan teachers as "leavers" when they move away from classroom teaching.

A NEW GENERATION OF EDUCATORS

The divergent career pathways found in the UCLA sample are not unique. Rather, they appear to be indicative of a "new generation" of teacher. The Harvard Project on the Next Generation of Teachers qualitatively studied a group of fifty first- and second-year Massachusetts public school teachers and found many of them approached their teaching job as "one of several in a series of careers they expect[ed] to have" (Moore Johnson et al. 2004, p. 28). As Susan Moore Johnson and her colleagues (2004) found, "Those who consider teaching today have an array of alternative career options, many offering greater social status, providing more comfortable work environments, and offering far higher pay than teaching" (p. 19). In short, they argue that a generational turn in the educational workforce is under way nationwide.

Consider the following statistics: nationwide, teachers currently make up only half of the education workforce. The other half includes instructional coordinators, aides, administrators, librarians, media specialists, school psychologists, speech pathologists, audiologists, social workers, attendance officers, cafeteria workers, custodians, bus drivers, and many more education-related jobs. Every year, 4 percent of the newest crop of teachers (those with less than five years of experience) decide to leave the classroom for one of these roles: this accounts for more than 25,000 young teachers who gain employment in the vast education workforce every year. Though the public hears a great deal about teachers leaving the classroom—the so-called teacher retention crisis—a nuanced account of where and why these teachers go rarely makes headlines.

Part of this story is captured by a startling national trend. Based on the U.S. National Center for Education Statistics Common Core Data, between 1992 and 2001, the number of *education staff* working in elementary and secondary public school systems in the United States grew by 25.4 percent—from 4.7 million up to 5.9 million. Yet of all role categories in education, *teachers* experienced the least growth, growing 3.5 percent less than expected if proportions had remained static, whereas other categories like district administration, instructional coordinators, and instructional aides outpaced their expected growth by between 13 percent and 14 percent. The high-poverty, low-performing schools in which UCLA graduates work are undoubtedly qualitatively different than the work-places of the majority of teachers in the nation. Given the additional student- and teacher-support personnel often required at these high-poverty, low-performing schools— such as after-school program coordinators, bilingual coor-dinators, parent outreach coordinators, reading and curriculum specialists, or beginning teacher support providers—well-qualified teachers with master's degrees, such as those profiled here, are looked to as teacher lead-ers, often pulled from their classrooms to serve in the above-mentioned roles. Our data suggests that such teachers have myriad opportunities to move from the classroom into another role within the school or district. Although these limited workforce categories provide lim-ited information about the nature of nonteaching profes-sional roles and may differ by school and district, the fact that they are outpacing teaching warrants careful atten-tion by the profession and the public.

One argument that might be offered in support of this trend is that by creating layers of support personnel within the system, the job of teaching is further profes-sionalized: fewer teachers are better supported to do their job well. Another less compelling argument is that alternative pathways enable career development and ad-vancement, thus benefiting individuals and keeping well-prepared educators in the system, if not in class-rooms. But at what cost? This is a complex question, and yet there are some basic costs to students that we can and should consider. If our study population is representative of well-prepared teachers nationwide, then the career movement in and out of nonteaching roles is a phenomenon that potentially affects the majority of well-prepared teachers over time. Students experience this movement as a direct loss of well-prepared teachers, often coupled with exposure to the new, less experienced teachers who fill the vacancies they leave behind. Granted, this loss may translate into support for other teachers who are able to thereby improve their practice, but the extent to which this benefit outweighs the direct cost to students is rarely scrutinized. *The retention literature focuses on the costs of attrition to the system and schools, assuming that a net loss at either level decreases the quality of education for students. When we expand this policy frame to include role changers or "shifters" as a retention category, the question becomes more complicated: does attrition from teaching into other education roles increase or decrease the overall quality of education for students?*

Focus point

Intense political debate surrounding the "bureaucratic bloat" and effectiveness of our public education system often clouds even-handed and accurate analysis of this trend. Some critics of the system, for example, use national workforce data to lob charges of self-serving inefficiency based on the ratio of teachers to other educational professionals. Meanwhile, some within the system respond that never before have schools been asked to do so much, and therefore, the purported "bloat," if it exists at all, is both justifiable and necessary. Instead of probing the value of nonteaching educational roles, the debate is often polarized by adherence to bureaucratic centralization on one end and radical decentralization on the other. Our own research allows us to probe the value of teaching and nonteaching roles in urban education from the perspective of those living them. As we recount in later chapters, educators understand the tradeoffs between staying in and leaving the classroom, and they grapple with what it means for students as well as the larger project to promote change across the educational system.

CAREER CYCLES

Along with laying bare the array of career possibilities in education, research on teachers' careers also gives us an understanding of the effect of time on these careers. After a few years teaching, several teachers we talked with spoke of having "plateaued" and therefore found themselves "stagnating" or "idling" in their work. They began to wonder if, for them, teaching as a career had run its course. Furthermore, several teachers had come to believe that their initial professional goals could be better met if they shifted into other realms of education work, and that shifting would enable them to effect broader changes in education. For example, one teacher talked about "starting to feel like [my contribution] has to go beyond just 20 kids a year." Another talked about her professional impact having to be "much bigger than just being a good teacher." A third talked about "going back to [that idea of] social justice: how I can do more than just with my 20 students—where I can go next?" Although we explore these career aspirations in depth in the following chapters, it is important at the outset to understand them in the bigger picture of human development, life stages, and career cycles in the teaching profession.

Many researchers posit a career cycle to the profession of teaching (see, for example, Fessler and Christensen 1992; Huberman 1994; Sikes, Measor, and Woods 1985). *By a career cycle, we mean that researchers have found that most teachers travel through somewhat predictable phases as they move along in their teaching career. Each phase carries with it particular sets of professional and personal concerns, needs, satisfactions, and perspectives.*

Focus point

Most career models posit beginning, middle, and late stages to one's career in teaching. Generally, the early career phases are marked by survival concerns (such as learning how to operate the copy machine or just emotionally make it through the school day), a socialization into the values of the school and profession, and various kinds of beginning teacher difficulties (like classroom management and teacher paperwork). The middle phases are marked by high degrees of confidence, success, and a desire to broaden one's impact. Many of the teachers we studied fit well into these beginning and middle career phases. Late career phases are marked by a kind of winding down, an elder's kindly affection toward students and newer teachers, and an either serene or bitter gradual disengagement from the profession.

Michael Huberman (1989, 1994) conducted extensive research on career cycles for a group of teachers in Switzerland. He reported that after three to five years in teaching, many teachers began to "stabilize" and then became more activist and innovative in their work and/or reassessed their career choices. This stabilization phase could be perceived by ambitious, talented teaching professionals as a plateau or kind of stagnation. If, however, as Huberman found, this temporary phase of stabilization over a year's time often yields to subsequent cycles of experimentation/activism characterized by new levels of professional growth, along with satisfaction in teaching, we might consider the possibility that some "shifters" who are experiencing genuine impatience might find—given time, additional roles, and varied professional development opportunities—new challenges and satisfactions without having to leave the classroom.

Career cycles also map onto more general developmental cycles of life and work. The idealism of youth over time gives way to more "adult" concerns such as pragmatism, cynicism, status, and financial support for one's self and family. For example, a teacher when young, single, and without kids is more willing to give 60–70 energetic hours a week to teaching than she will eight years later with a spouse, children, and other diverse commitments. As extensive research in occupational sociology documents, our work lives follow somewhat predictable patterns with age.

CONCLUSION

We offer this brief landscape of careers in education as a backdrop for the personalized career stories to come. We have contrasted two teaching traditions to characterize and distinguish the identity of the change-minded educators we studied. We also provided a brief overview of our longitudinal data in order to map out the vast array of opportunities and career pathways available to change-minded educators. This data helped portray the changing nature of the educational workforce and the next generation of teachers. In closing, we offered a brief glimpse into the research on career cycles, recognizing the powerful role that time, maturation, and life circumstances play in career development.

In the next three chapters, you will meet seven "new generation," change-minded educators, hear about their career decisions, and learn from their professional actions and reactions. Through their stories, you will see how these individuals make sense of their careers by way of their connections to other people—by responding to others' personal and professional needs and, in turn, feeling valued, nurtured, and supported by these colleagues, students, and family members. Finally, you will witness their stories unfolding against the larger landscape of careers in education. You will see how the traditions of teaching intersect to guide individual career decisions. You will notice individuals navigating a vast array of possible career opportunities and struggling to reconcile the effects of each. And you will observe this group of educators begin to grapple with the effects of aging, parenting, and maturation in their lives, and how they weigh those factors alongside their career goals and social commitments. Let us now turn to the stories of our seven educators and the struggles involved as they attempt to shape, and are in turn shaped by, the world of urban education.

DISCUSSION QUESTIONS

1. Why did you enter the teaching profession? Are these initial reasons for entry still relevant for you? If you have been teaching for a while, have your motivations for teaching changed?

2. Does the tradition of teaching as low-status work affect your own sense of professional identity and satisfaction, and if so, how? Are there other cultural traditions that more accurately capture your own professional identity and satisfaction?

3. Where are you in your own career cycle? How have maturation and life changes influenced your work as an educator?

4. What opportunities exist in your school, district, or state for extending your work beyond the classroom? If you are just entering teaching, what are the workplace conditions that will help you feel both supported and challenged? How will you seek out and identify these conditions during the job search process?

FURTHER READING

Huberman, Michael. 1994. *The Lives of Teachers*. New York: Teachers College Press.

Kohl, Herbert R. 1998. *The Discipline of Hope: Learning from a Lifetime of Teaching*. New York: New Press.

Oakes, Jeannie, and Martin Lipton. 2006. *Teaching to Change the World*. New York: McGraw-Hill.

Quartz, Karen H., and TEP Research Group. 2003. "Too Angry to Leave: Supporting New Teachers' Commitment to Transform Urban Schools." *Journal of Teacher Education* 54(2): 99–111.

NOTE

1. Although this sample is slightly skewed to earlier career teachers, the only notable discrepancy occurs in the eighth and ninth years, where under-representation can reasonably be attributed to the smaller cell size and the probability of nonresponse after so many years out of the program.

CHAPTER TWO

EXERCISING PROFESSIONAL AUTONOMY

ONE OF THE HALLMARKS of professionals is their judgment. Based on specialized training, knowledge, and a critical understanding of contexts and individuals, we trust professionals to use their judgment in deciding which drug to prescribe, which legal precedent to invoke, or which building design to use. Professionals earn credentials, signaling to the broader culture that they are trustworthy. As their careers develop, professionals also earn increased distinctions that signify mastery and accomplishment. As a profession, teaching has all of this. Additionally, the No Child Left Behind Act has made teacher certification a priority in order to ensure that all students are taught by a "highly qualified" teacher; most states officially "tenure" teachers after they have spent three to five years teaching on a probationary status; and the National Board for Professional Teaching Standards awards certification to accomplished teachers. Why, then, do so many teachers leave the profession, lamenting that it provides little opportunity to exercise professional autonomy and judgment? We begin by framing the history, structures, and culture that define the quest for professional autonomy and then turn to Armando, Barbara,

Christine, and Diana to learn more about how this quest is enacted across a variety of career pathways.

FRAMING THE COMPLEXITY: WHAT IS PROFESSIONAL AUTONOMY AND WHY IS IT IMPORTANT?

The literature on teacher development and careers is rife with research and stories about the importance of a teacher's sense of—variously put—*autonomy, efficacy*, or *control over one's work* on the teacher's professional satisfaction (Fessler and Christensen 1992; Sarason 1990; Sikes, Measor, and Woods 1985). These studies point to the fact that many teachers who have undergone specialized preparation and possess at least a few years of experience should have, want to have, or deserve to have the freedom to make decisions and have increasing amounts of control in their work. *When you have limited professional autonomy, your expertise can feel slighted and your ability to educate students unfairly fettered. This, not surprisingly, can lead to disappointment, frustration, and burnout—the physical and emotional consequences of working very hard with little control over your work yet considerable responsibility for its outcomes.* It is at that point that many educators consider other positions in education that seem to offer more autonomy while retaining—or even increasing—the social impact of their work. To understand why it is so hard to achieve professional autonomy as a teacher, we map out four dimensions of autonomy and describe how they fit within the broader profession of education.

Focus point

Preparation

A teacher who has been well trained is a highly qualified professional who deserves the freedom and control to exercise his or her expertise appropriately. We see this conception in much of the research on teacher professionalization (Engvall 1997; Holmes Group 1986; National Commission on Teaching and America's Future 2003), which argues that teachers should be rigorously prepared and then given the autonomy to teach as they see fit, provided they are held in some way accountable for their role in student achievement. This dimension of professional autonomy also forms a common criticism of the recent policy culture in education—of which the No Child Left Behind Act is one current, public face. The criticism is that if we are requiring our teachers to be well prepared and licensed before they can teach—to be denoted as "highly qualified" professionals—then we should not at the same time decrease their autonomy by mandating exactly what they are to teach, how they will teach it, and by what means student learning will be measured (Samway and Pease-Alvarez 2005; Meier and Wood 2004). Many teachers who consider themselves professionals expect corresponding levels of autonomy in their daily work.

Competence, Status, and Respect

A second dimension of professional autonomy relates to competence, status, and respect in teaching generally, and urban teaching, specifically (Herbst 1989; Weiner 2005). Connected to, but different from, control over your work is the question of whether others acknowledge and respect your professional competence as a teacher. None of us likes to be continually ignored or—worse—criticized when we believe we are doing good, valuable work. As teachers, we hope students recognize our talents and efforts. We hope their parents appreciate it too. We also expect commensurate recognition from supervisors, peers, and from larger communities such as professional organizations and society as a whole. If a teacher is highly competent, he or she often possesses a corresponding confidence; that confidence leads to a sense that others should recognize it as well and, in turn, offer both a corresponding level of professional freedom and institutionalized respect. Though few teachers enter the profession solely to garner these kinds of ego-driven accolades, over time, without those kudos, we sometimes wonder if all the hard work is worth it.

Pedagogical Position

Many educators and education researchers believe that classroom teachers—being closest to the students and knowing their talents, needs, and individual contexts—are the ones best positioned to make decisions related to teaching and learning. This kind of decentralized approach to education runs counter to the "one size fits all" perspective inherent in most standardized or top-down school reforms. Instead, it argues that local communities have unique features, as do individual students and particular classroom populations. It is the well-prepared and competent teacher, therefore, who is best positioned to diagnose student needs, fashion appropriate learning opportunities, and measure student growth and learning. This dimension of professional autonomy corresponds to a long history of teaching with roots in student-centered instruction (Piaget 1954; Fosnot 1996), funds of knowledge (Moll 1988; González, Moll, and Amanti 2005), action research (Cochran-Smith and Lytle 1999), and culturally relevant pedagogy (Gay 2000; Ladson-Billings 1995). Many teachers find that current teaching mandates, standardized tests, and prescriptive curricula are ill-fitted to the particularities of their students. This is especially true in urban schools with their layers upon layers of bureaucracy, reform initiatives, and public scrutiny. The vast separation between those who create teaching policies and materials, on the one hand, and those who actually know and work with students, on the other, disturbs many teachers. This current reality leads some teachers to conclude their work in the classroom is too constraining for them to make the kind of difference they desire. And they likewise come to believe it is bad for children. These "pushes" out of the classroom—as is the case for some of the teachers profiled in this chapter— sometimes encourage teachers to leave teaching for positions in education where they, themselves, can create and disseminate curriculum or policy.

Development and Growth

A fourth dimension of professional autonomy relates to teachers developing and changing in identifiable ways over the course of their teaching career. Many researchers posit a career cycle to the profession of teaching. As we described in Chapter 1, a career cycle is the set of somewhat predictable stages that most teachers travel through as they move along in their teaching careers. Of particular note here is that when teachers get to their middle career stage (sometimes as early as three or four years out, sometimes closer to six or seven), many of them are hitting their stride. They have professional comfort, confidence, and mastery. There is a generation of more novice teachers below them, and so they have some seniority. They often find themselves teaching younger siblings of students they had previously taught, so there is a history to their practice. This midcareer stage often produces in a teacher the belief that he or she warrants a high degree of professional autonomy and, in fact, *requires* increased autonomy to remain challenged, energized, and useful. This means that middle-career teachers who believe they aren't experiencing appropriate levels of autonomy may be at particularly great risk of leaving teaching.

This multidimensional concept of professional autonomy helps determine the career pathways of teachers working to change schools. Many classroom teachers— especially the teachers we studied with specialized training and those at midcareer locations on the career cycle—might fairly expect professional autonomy in their

Cross-Reference
See Book 5, Chapter 2, for discussions of teacher leadership in schools and communities.

work. Yet public school teachers across the United States report having limited input into schoolwide social and instructional decisions such as curriculum, tracking, and discipline policies (Yee 1990; Ingersoll 2003). This is especially true for teachers at large, comprehensive public schools like those most often found in urban high-poverty areas. Large urban schools tend to have highly centralized bureaucracies, resulting in hierarchical settings in which educators face limited amounts of autonomy and constrained teacher participation and stakeholder collaboration (Weiner 2005). Teachers at large urban schools report having less influence over key workplace decisions than teachers at smaller public schools, and the current push for accountability compounds this situation. In hard-to-staff schools where students struggle to master basic skills, professional judgment and autonomy for teachers are often seen as scarce luxury goods. This fact contributes to the view of teaching as a low-status occupation and fuels teacher attrition.

Focus point

Although many of the teachers we studied did leave the classroom, most remained in education. *These are educators committed to changing the world through education and working with historically disadvantaged populations of children. They may be attracted to other positions in education, and they are certainly sensitive to pressures around material benefits, personal satisfaction, intellectual challenges, and the working conditions of their jobs, but we found they were always doing their job calculus around their core commitments to education, kids, and social change.* Let's turn to their stories.

STORIES

Armando: Moving Up the Ladder, with Reservations

Armando intended a career in civil rights law in order to help people like those from his own working-class Latino community before shifting into education. He continues to use his core commitments as a kind of anchor around which other factors of his career development twist and turn. Having taught for a few years, he was invited out of the classroom by his school administrator, who was moving to the district office and invited him to join the ranks of administration. It is not surprising that a talented, well-prepared, successful, young bilingual Latino teacher might be invited into a leadership position even if he had only been teaching for three and a half years. The administrator who invited him may have believed Armando could better serve students as a school administrator. Perhaps she was also responding to a need to diversify the administrative ranks with talented educators of color. In fact, this fits a pattern in which talented beginning educators of color are invited into leadership positions early and quickly—creating a fast track up the hierarchy (and, presumably, away from students). Supporting and grooming for administrative positions those educators who have backgrounds commensurate with many urban school students may combine good educational practice with politically advantageous district leadership and culturally responsible hiring practices. And yet we suspect that this phenomenon carries with it both benefits and detriments.

Armando wondered if he was pulled out of teaching too early. He told us,

> One of the reasons why I feel as if it was a mistake to come out of the classroom [so soon] is because a lot of times I feel incompetent [as a principal]. Not that I'm a stupid person, but because I just don't have the time to concentrate on this job solely to learn a lot of the nuances that a lot of people already have by virtue of working here for many, many years.

Later, when we asked him what advice he might have for other urban teachers, he did not hesitate:

I would definitely suggest staying in the classroom a little bit longer. If they've been in the classroom for a while
then I think they would have a sufficient knowledge and
experience base to draw upon [as a school administra-
tor]. If not, I would suggest staying there a little bit
more. Don't be in such a rush.

He also reported that he has concerns about talented
teachers being directed into administration for the
teacher void it leaves behind:

**"I think the best
teachers are
always tapped
on the shoulder
to become an
administrator."**

Being tapped on the shoulder [and invited into adminis-
tration] is problematic. I think it pulls the best teachers
out of the classroom. I think the best teachers are always
tapped on the shoulder to become an administrator. It's
almost like there's this vacuum. Where do all the administrators go when they leave the school? Why is there always such a need for an administrator? I think the best
teachers are always likely to become administrators and
they are taken away from the classroom. And in that
sense I think it impacts education in a negative way, to
the detriment of the students in the school.

Armando shifted into school administration because
of a convergence of factors. He was "tapped on the
shoulder"—identified as a strong educator and invited
up the professional hierarchy into an administrative position. This provided some additional prestige—one aspect
of professional autonomy—and a higher salary. He also
told us he craved the learning and personal growth a new
position would offer him. Most important to him, Armando believed the shift into administration offered a
way to better improve educational opportunities for the
kinds of students he cares about:

When you're a teacher, you're frustrated about some of
the things that occur outside of your classroom—

schoolwide—that you think could be done better, and
you wish were done better, and at times you get so frustrated that you want to become an administrator. In
fact, some of us do—because we want to change a lot of
those things. . . . I perceived that there was potential to
establish a better learning environment for students, for
the [working-class, Latino] students that I identify with,
having grown up the same way. And I remember all the
time what it was like for me growing up and how I
struggled in school, and how alienated I felt and how
alienated my parents felt, and I just didn't want that for
a lot of the kids. I wanted to change that, and that was
the carrot for me to go into administration.

At the time Armando was invited into administration, he
believed that, as much as teachers could accomplish in
their classrooms, there were outside factors that limited
teachers' work and therefore students' opportunities to
learn. He believed that school administrators worked
from a position of broader autonomy and efficacy and so
could improve schooling conditions which, in turn,
would support teachers working with students to a
greater degree. Simply put, he felt he could make more
of a difference as an administrator.

And yet, a few years after having made that shift, Armando was not convinced of administrators' autonomy
and efficacy. "At times I really don't know why I'm doing
this job. I feel like a middle manager. I'm given directives
about what I am to do, regardless of what I believe should
be done. I feel almost at times that I'm a robot, and in that
sense it's frustrating and lacks meaning." Armando found
that the institutional constraints, the time devoted to the
minutiae of school administration (which he variously described as "administrivia," "plate-spinning," and "paper
pushing"), and the absence of cooperation by many teachers and fellow administrators have led him to believe that
he may have less autonomy than he did as a teacher.

A tradeoff emerges: teachers often have more influence on students but over a smaller domain (the classroom), whereas school administrators have less direct influence on students but over a larger domain (the school). On good days Armando still believes he is making a profound difference in the lives of kids, and he believes he will grow as an administrator and make even more of a difference in the future. But on the other days (and it seems like, according to him, these comprise the majority), he is less hopeful. In general, he returns to the following point: "The longer I'm away from the classroom, the less I feel as if I'm making a difference. There are days where I feel I do, but on a regular basis, I don't. It's frustrating." Summarizing his dilemma, Armando said this:

> I think when you're a teacher, you impact lives a little bit more directly, at least that's what it feels like, because you see the students every day, and you're able to touch base with them every day, and I think they open up to you a little bit more, because you're not seen as the heavy—the vice principal or the principal in charge of discipline. You tend to foster closer relationship in that sense, and that in turn impacts their lives both academically and socially. . . . When you become an administrator, you want to change those things but find that it's not as easy as you might have thought. In many schools, there is an entrenched school culture; you have to be really pragmatic about how you introduce change. It feels very frustrating in terms of effecting change as an administrator because you have to be a politician. I mean, you have to get buy-in from all the stakeholders, not just teachers but all the stakeholders, and progress is—the impact is—more delayed. At times there is incredible change that takes place, such as restructuring the whole school, but most of the time it just feels like you're pushing paper. You have a boss who will be gone in two or three years, and another one comes in who

then tries to effect change. But by the time something actually starts happening they're gone too, and so forth.

Further complicating the equation of his professional autonomy and satisfaction in relation to the personal and professional costs of his job is that Armando believes returning to the classroom as a teacher is no longer a viable option. He has ruled that out because he has become accustomed to the extra money, and due to some life changes—namely, caring for aging parents—he cannot afford to forgo the additional salary a school principal earns. This puts him in a bind: his core commitments require him to stay in education, though he is not certain he will remain in an administrative position and does not believe he will return to teaching. When we asked him what else he is contemplating, Armando reported that he may consider combining his law school education with his commitments to students to find a job working with Latino students and families confronting suspensions and other school-related legal appeals. But for now he feels a little trapped because moving into school administration has not offered him the professional autonomy—that freedom and control to make a difference—that he seeks.

POSSIBLE ROLE IN EDUCATION: EDUCATIONAL ADVOCATE

Many legal organizations exist that advocate on behalf of students and families. For example, the Education Law Center in Philadelphia is an advocacy organization that works to "make good public education a reality for Pennsylvania's most vulnerable students: poor children, children of color, kids with disabilities, English-language learners, children in foster homes and institutions, and others" (http://www.elc-pa.org).

Barbara: Shifting and Climbing to Be Heard

Barbara is one of six children of working-class Latino parents and the first in her family to attend college. While in college, Barbara was interested in making professional use of her English-Spanish bilingualism, but thought it would be within a career in political science or engineering. However, volunteering in a bilingual classroom and observing the teacher flatly ignoring Spanish-speaking students in favor of the English speakers, she decided that Latino students needed her:

> Seeing what happened in that classroom made me feel like, "Wait a minute! Those [Spanish speakers] deserve as much of an education as any other student!" And so I suddenly wanted to help other Latinos, and not let schools believe that, because these students only spoke Spanish, they couldn't learn.

This experience motivated a shift in her undergraduate studies: she switched to major in Spanish and minor in education. Upon graduation, Barbara entered the UCLA Teacher Education Program and afterward began teaching first grade in a bilingual classroom at a high-poverty, predominantly Latino Los Angeles public school. Given the mostly antibilingual sentiment in California education, Barbara had to find a school with either a Waiver-to-Basic or a Dual Immersion program in order to teach in a bilingual classroom. She enjoyed her first years teaching at this school. She liked the children, she found the principal supportive and smart, and there were myriad opportunities for professional development and collaboration among teachers. However, after a few years, once the principal had left and much of the professional development disappeared, her teaching joy faded. These changes coincided with the Los Angeles Unified School District (LAUSD) adopting a mandated reading program for elementary schools called Open

Court—a scripted reading approach many progressive educators consider overly prescriptive in its learning and frustratingly constraining in its pedagogy. *Open Court Reading* (published by SRA/McGraw-Hill) is a prepackaged, scripted, pre-K–6 language arts program based on explicit phonemic awareness, employed mostly in low-performing schools. Supporters find it an effective research-based solution to underachievement; critics consider it expensive, overly rigid, and rarely successful. Los Angeles Unified School District has adopted Open Court in all but its highest-performing schools.

As Open Court took hold at the school where Barbara taught, she came to believe that teachers—especially equity-minded teachers like her who advocated for and taught English-language learners—were not being heard within education policy circles. Open Court's constraining function on Barbara's professional autonomy was a kind of final straw that led her to think it was time to consider finding a new role in education. While teaching, she had earned a master's degree in principal leadership during evenings, weekends, and summer, because she believed that principled school principals were needed in order to stand up to increasingly misguided policy mandates: "I know there's a big need for good teachers, but at the same time, with all the bureaucracy, with all the mandating-this and mandating-that, and the rise of high-stakes testing—I feel that more [school] principals are needed [in order] to say, 'Wait a minute! We need to stress learning, not testing.'"

After six years in the classroom, Barbara was simultaneously being pulled out of teaching and pushed into another education role—a gradual movement away from the classroom toward other kinds of education work. As a teacher, she had been appointed grade-level cochair at her school, which, in turn, led to a position as the teachers' union representative at her school. These assignments subtly shifted her focus from her classroom of students to whole groups of teachers at the school. As well, her teacher preparation experience had encouraged her to always consider the "big picture" in education: to see that classroom realities were reciprocally influenced by school, community, and larger sociopolitical contexts. As she moved out of her early career phase of teaching, she began to feel successful and confident, and yet unheard—this is where the pull intersected with the push. These interconnected experiences caused her to view educational administration as a "logical next step." The pushes out of the classroom were mostly about professional autonomy: she was searching for a way to make a bigger difference and had come to believe that teachers' work was becoming circumscribed more and more tightly as a result of the policy climate in education. Barbara had concluded that teachers are not well positioned within the network of education decision makers to confront disagreeable teaching policies, and that they—and the English-language learners many teachers in LAUSD serve—needed advocates to speak on their behalf. She had become dejected:

> This whole cookie-cutter model is frustrating. Even English-language development had become about having to give a language assessment every six weeks. Everything where teachers once had an avenue for creativity is being shut down. And, basically, these assessments [presume] that the teachers must be idiots—that we need scripts to tell us what to do. And then people complain that teachers aren't motivated?! Well, why would you want to do what they tell you to do when they don't treat you like a professional?

She wanted to be the kind of advocate she believed teachers needed. But whereas Armando shifted directly from teaching to become a vice principal, Barbara moved into administration incrementally. During the time of our research, she had just accepted a position as a program adviser coordinating Title 1.

POSSIBLE ROLE IN EDUCATION: TITLE I COORDINATOR

Title I is a federal program designed to improve the academic achievement of the disadvantaged (i.e., limited-English-proficient and low-income students) by offering supplemental funding that supports their learning. Title I coordinators work for school districts and manage the funds and educational programs associated with this federal initiative. For information, see http://www.ed.gov/policy/elsec/leg/esea02/pg1.html.

Barbara says that she plans to do this job for two years and then become either a vice principal or language acquisition specialist:

I think my definition of what it means to be professionally successful will change with each step. It will be unique to the position I'm in. Recently, feeling successful as a teacher had been in regard to my students. As a coordinator, it's about the students and teachers. But in other positions, like if I take a language specialist position or a position downtown, then I'm not going to be working with students, or even with teachers as much, so [my view of whom I'm supposed to represent] is going to change.

Barbara's goal is to find a professional location from which she can confront what she considers to be bad education policy. When we pointed out to her that she is planning to leave classroom teaching while simultaneously telling us she is currently the happiest she has ever been as a teacher, she discussed the constrained autonomy of teachers:

Yes, I know, but honestly—I go to these [district] meetings, and you see teachers who are just sitting there, not saying anything [critical]. And when a teacher does speak out and says, "You know what? This [Open Court reading] program is not working. Why would you spend millions of dollars on this?" . . . none of the higher-ups even hear her, you know? People might listen a bit—they'll nod their heads—but then they'll say, "OK, you've had your five minutes. Let's get on with the meeting." And it's like, "Wait a minute! We're here for the kids; we're not here for the governor; we're not here for these superintendents. We're here for the students." I feel that by going up [into administration], I'm going to have more of a voice than as a teacher.

Barbara is searching for a position from which she can create real change that genuinely supports teachers working with English-language learners in a pedagogically appropriate manner. Yet, she is also predicting personal and material benefits from shifting out of teaching into administration. She told us that she did not mind such a time-intensive job as urban teaching (she reported working over fifty hours a week, attending professional development over her breaks) because she was single and without children of her own. But with the planning of her wedding over the summer, Barbara had begun to consider the difficulties of being a committed teacher, spouse, and mother. (Armando, however, would tell her that an administrator's schedule is no walk in the park!) Barbara said that when she does have kids of her own, she plans to stop working for a few years and then return to education—very likely as a teacher, she predicted, until her children are older, when she would then return to educational administration. She also talked about salary factors:

I've taught for five and a half years. I'm at the top of the [teachers'] salary scale now, so it's like, "OK, where do I go from here?" Salary is an issue because, for the amount of education that I have, I should be making a lot more money. . . . I didn't go into teaching for the money, and I'm not making these [career] changes for the money. I'm doing it primarily to feel that I'm making a difference. But I'm also thinking that I need to take care of myself, because these kids are not going to maintain me, for sure.

Barbara's example illustrates the complex, intertwined factors that influence a teacher's staying in, shifting in, or leaving the profession. Her experience suggests that schools that offer increased autonomy to teachers as they develop into middle-career professionals will better retain them in the classroom (as well as capitalize on their valuable insights into teaching and learning). *In Barbara's case, had she been offered increased and authentic opportunities to collaborate with education administrators and work with teachers and curriculum developers (not on top of her teaching work, but replacing some of it), she may have remained in teaching longer.* She believed that the education structure was mostly top-down: that powerful noneducators unfamiliar with her community and her students were mandating teaching approaches that did not fit. She believed that those with power in education were not listening to teachers—the professionals best positioned to advise on teaching policies. She was also not immune to issues of workload and financial remuneration. These personal and professional concerns are guiding her career path up the traditional educational hierarchy.

Focus point

Christine: Studying How to Make Change

Christine's first teaching placement was in a large, urban middle school. At this school, she experienced "disconnected administrators who didn't really know what it was like to be in the classroom" and a faculty that almost never worked together. As Christine explained, "We tried, but nothing really stuck," which is common in

schools with high rates of annual teacher turnover. The
negative impact of that turnover interfered with Christine's work right from the start when, two months into
her first year, her partner teacher abruptly quit. The two
had accepted their jobs together with a guarantee that
they would team-teach the same cohort of sixth-grade
students: Christine would focus on language arts while
her partner teacher would cover math and science. In
this way, they expected jurisdiction over the classroom
instruction their students received. However, this
arrangement was undermined by the sudden departure
of her partner teacher and by the intrusion of myriad
program mandates, curricular requirements, administrative initiatives, and standardized assessment demands.

To fill the resulting teacher vacancy, the school hired
what Christine described as an "awful" long-term substitute who stayed for one month, then another substitute who finished out the year before leaving. Christine
therefore spent her first year in the classroom working
side by side with a string of temporary teachers. This
pattern continued over the following two years, with the
school hiring woefully underprepared beginning teachers or long-term substitutes who came and went. Trying
to teach in this situation and simultaneously mentor
these teachers was a physically and emotionally exhaust-
ing task, and Christine knew her students were not
learning much. The situation also precluded any kind of
collaborative teaching situation—the reason she joined
the school in the first place. After the third year, Christine decided to leave, explaining to us that "I didn't feel
like I fit."

This lack of fit between Christine and her workplace
was largely a misalignment between the vision that
Christine had of herself as a teacher and the reality of her
work conditions. The fact that Christine could not fulfill
the vision of her professional self is not uncommon
among new teachers, since they are frequently still
searching for a sense of who they ultimately want to

become professionally. Christine's situation is less common, though. Not only did she have a fairly well-developed vision of her teaching goals upon entering the profession, but she also had come to believe that achieving such a vision was impossible in the context where she was working. For Christine, being a successful teacher meant working closely with others on behalf of students: this was something that the institutional instabilities of this large, chaotic school appeared to prohibit.

The concept of fit was like a compass for Christine as she searched for a new place to work. She ultimately chose a Los Angeles charter middle school in its second year of operation because she believed her vision and core commitments could be met at a school that was new, explicitly focused on innovation, and relatively small:

> I thought I would have the opportunity to be more involved in teaching progressive curriculum and maybe increase the level of collegiality from zero to at least something. . . . The school wanted to do progressive things, to reach out. Because it was a smaller environment, I thought we could support kids better.

But this new situation proved disappointing. During her first year there, Christine realized that her strong commitment to marginalized students was not shared throughout the school. The principal noticed this too and offered her a job working offsite with a group of expelled students. Christine accepted and found herself working with a small class of students in the basement of a church under construction. She found the work invigorating and useful, yet overwhelming. She could teach the way she wanted—integrating subject matter across disciplines, engaging students in learning projects, building strong relationships with students and families. But there were tradeoffs: she was isolated from her colleagues and given almost no support. As meaningful as she believed the work was, Christine ultimately felt she could not keep it up: "I realized I had no help, no resources, no one to follow up except me. It was not sustainable." Although Christine had found professional autonomy in this teaching situation, she had not found professional support—proving the point that autonomy by itself is merely isolation.

Within a week of leaving the charter school, Christine was hired to work in an alternative school for students expelled from the local district. The physical conditions were not much better than the windowless, stuffy church basement from before, but she was thrilled by the opportunity to do the work she loved within a formal structure that provided both resources and administrative support. She appreciated working closely with a smaller number of kids and felt a great sense of reward but soon found that her practice remained relatively isolated from that of other teachers, and again the exhaustion of working alone took its toll: "I felt I made a difference, but at a huge cost for me." These experiences encouraged Christine to reflect on her commitments—the vision she had of herself as an educator, the kind of impact she wanted to have, and the manner and degree to which all these matched the conditions of existing education institutions. This period of reflection was about how to balance notions of professional autonomy against both the need for support and a way to authentically enact her core commitments. She concluded that the working conditions in urban schools in Los Angeles did not allow her to be successful— a self-reassessment that led to a return to graduate school because, as she explains, "I couldn't find a school where I had allies and wasn't an outsider."

Christine's story raises several issues related to professional autonomy and urban teaching. She was professionally prepared to teach in ways designed to effect social change and was encouraged to think of teaching as inherently collaborative. Outside the university setting,

"I felt I made a difference, but at a huge cost for me."

however, she found that this was not so easy. Large urban schools have an institutional force of their own—one that has over time congealed into webs of entrenched bureaucracies, rules, management techniques, impersonal procedures, and standardized practices. These constraints work against any individual, alone or with allies, hoping to make change. Additionally, Christine realized that autonomy in its extreme is actually seclusion. For teachers to have the autonomy to teach as they see fit and yet feel successful, their professional freedom must be complemented by support and like-minded collaborators. Christine learned this the hard way.

Christine's story also raises the option of returning to graduate school as an often attractive pathway for teachers feeling burned out. The university setting typically offers education students and faculty great autonomy over their work in settings that can be as collaborative (or as independent) as one would like. But for change-minded educators like Christine, graduate school is a means to an end—not an end in itself. Based on her core commitments to children, Christine expects to use her Ph.D. studies to facilitate a return to K–12 education so she can continue working toward student achievement in high-poverty communities. When we last talked with Christine, she had completed her first year as a doctoral student and was weighing her future options. She was considering becoming a school principal, or perhaps conducting research on how to improve education in urban locations. Most important, she was using graduate school to better understand how to find a place where she "fits." For Christine, returning to graduate school was a way to learn about the larger landscape of urban schooling and develop a strategy for change. Once she completes her graduate degree Christine expects to be better equipped to return to the K–12 system, find a role that fits her, and become the kind of successful educator she longs to be.

Diana: Finding Satisfaction Within
and Beyond the Classroom

Diana has taught kindergarten in the same school—in
the same classroom even—since she began her teaching
career a decade ago. She said she knew she wanted to be a
teacher ever since high school. She grew up in Los Angeles during a violent time and reports that she saw teaching as a way to "be a part of the solution."

> I grew up in LA at the height of the whole gang
> thing—the Bloods and the Crips—and I remember in
> high school there was also a lot of tension between the
> black and Korean communities: a girl had been shot
> about some orange juice; I remember this very vividly.
> So when I was in high school, I felt like education was
> very important. I just felt like there was so much work
> to be done, and my heart was really touched. I wanted
> to get in there to see if I could do something to make a
> difference.

Although Diana studied education and earned a
teaching credential in college in Washington, D.C., she
did not feel adequately prepared to teach upon graduation, so she entered UCLA's Teacher Education Program
to earn her master's degree and a California teaching credential. Ever since, she has remained closely connected
to UCLA's various teacher education, professional development, and community outreach networks. She has co-
facilitated UCLA-sponsored inquiry groups for teachers,
edited the local *Teaching to Change LA* online journal,
cotaught a class with a UCLA professor, and participated
in other projects and activities connected to the university. She has also taken two different leaves from her job
and done all of this while remaining a Los Angeles Unified School District kindergarten classroom teacher.

The first leave was a professional sabbatical she
learned about because "I read my contract really closely!

Several times over. Our district has this unique thing in the contract where you could be enrolled in a graduate program or do an independent study to benefit the district." What initiated this sabbatical was a confluence of factors:

> I really enjoy my teaching—probably to a fault, I think. And I wouldn't say I was necessarily at my burnout stage but I think, particularly, like I said, I had started some work with the parents of my students, and I wanted to take it further. And we had had some administrative changes which produced a lot of upheaval in the school community. So those factors would probably have been more of a push to get me out of there than necessarily [getting tired of] teaching, per se. It was a combination of things. I also did have real cause for taking time off because I had just had my son; I was a first-time parent, so there was that draw. The administrative changes and upheaval made me feel less guilty about leaving. And then . . . I was thinking about this sabbatical—you know, I had heard about the UCLA/IDEA [Institute for Democracy, Education, and Access] parent project in the past—and a peer of mine told me that the project was looking for people to work on it. And I thought, "This is it! This is my big break—a golden opportunity."

In this case, some initiative on her part, a flexible leave policy from the district, and a serendipitous professional development opportunity allowed Diana to simultaneously pursue new professional challenges, strike a desirable life-work balance, and remain committed to classroom teaching. The opportunity to be a "teacher-scholar" (see sidebar) enabled her to be with her new son, reconnect to the university she had previously attended, take a break from the daily rigors of teaching, and participate in a professional development project that nicely aligned with her core commitments and current teaching goals.

Diana returned to her classroom the next year reinvigorated, ready to implement the research she conducted on new ways of partnering with parents, and prepared to teach her colleagues what she had learned. Because of a leadership change, the administrative upheaval at her school had smoothed out. She had appreciated the chance to reconnect with educators whom she knew from her teacher education program.

POSSIBLE ROLE IN EDUCATION: TEACHER-SCHOLAR

Teacher-scholars engage in what is sometimes called "action research" or "teacher research." They choose educational questions that interest them, conduct research, and then apply what they learned to their own work. Opportunities for doing this kind of research are often available through local universities (e.g., UCLA's Institute for Democracy, Education, and Access, where Diana did her sabbatical), districts, or support organizations such as the Carnegie Academy for the Scholarship of Teaching and Learning in K–12 Education.

After a few more years teaching, Diana found herself again at a similar point in her career: she had no intention of leaving the classroom for good but wanted a break from the teaching routine and had a second child on the way. This time she combined her maternity leave with a significant amount of accrued vacation time and took an extended leave from her job. However, true to Diana's core commitments and her identity as a teacher, she found herself fitting some teaching work into her mothering role. She told us that she just couldn't stay away from teaching:

> When I would pass by a school, I'd automatically start thinking about teaching and children. And I think I

probably put it on a little thick with my own kids. I even ended up teaching a *Mommy and Me* class. I just voluntarily taught it; I didn't get any pay, but they needed a teacher. I just think teaching is in me.

Diana also did some work for a teaching colleague of hers who was coordinating union efforts in the school district. So, along with caring for her kids, Diana was stuffing envelopes and teaching parents.

These various professional experiences of Diana's— connected to but not the same as her teaching work— allowed her to find new challenges, grow professionally, and find some time for herself and her family. They offered her some control over her own teaching career and enabled her to view teaching as intellectually rewarding and flexible as well as socially meaningful. *Diana's story of autonomy, balance, and multiple roles points to the fact that some teachers will remain in the classroom when the circumstances of their teaching (in the contexts of their ever-changing lives) allow them to grow and find new professional challenges while also experiencing sufficient autonomy in their teaching work.* Diana remains optimistic about her teaching career and believes in her own ability to make a difference in the lives of children. Her varied education roles and her sense of professional autonomy have strengthened her love for teaching. This has resulted in an increased effectiveness not only with students but with their parents and other teachers, and it has allowed her to continue her work to improve districtwide conditions for teaching and learning. Professional autonomy, therefore, can also exist as a factor that retains classroom teachers who continue to find challenges, rewards, and meaning in their work. When teaching contexts provide increasing degrees of autonomy for teachers, continued opportunities for professional growth, and recognition of teachers' hard work and success, it appears that many teachers will remain in the profession longer.

Focus point

CONCLUSION: HOW CAN YOU BEST EXERCISE PROFESSIONAL AUTONOMY?

Reading about these teachers' experiences illuminates the multiple factors that uniquely combine to shape educators' decisions to stay in or shift out of classroom teaching. We hope both beginning and experienced teachers can locate themselves inside parts of these varied stories. All teachers must ask themselves the kinds of questions that will encourage wise decision making that acknowledges the multiple career factors, appreciates the complexity of education work, and maximizes both one's personal satisfaction and ability to make a difference in the lives of others. To conclude this chapter, we suggest three questions that relate to the four different facets of autonomy introduced in this chapter.

Is your work intellectually challenging? Inside the concept of professional autonomy is a continual push in one's work: an exciting, constant pressure to keep learning, to think hard and act well, and to be challenged to consider things in new ways. Absent that inherent drive for personal-professional growth, there is the unpleasant feeling of inertia. *This means that one important facet of increasing your autonomy as a developing teacher is paying attention to the developmental nature of teaching work.* A beginning teacher may define autonomy in terms of opportunities to teach freely but within the helpful scaffold of mentors, colleagues, and teaching supports. This phase is about *stabilizing*. After a few years of experience, however, this same teacher—now a midcareer teacher— probably conceives of professional autonomy more in terms of moving forward. This phase is about *growing*. For some, this movement forward propels them away from the classroom. For others, growth can be found inside the work of teaching.

Focus point

Diana told us that she is "the type of person that really gets a charge out of new learning, out of new experiences, having my brain challenged in a different way

periodically." She went on to say that her experience doing a year of professional development work allowed her
to "stretch" her thinking about education and then return to the classroom: "I was really excited about this
new learning that's so applicable to what I was returning
to—sort of like, 'OK, now I've had this [research oppor-
tunity]; now I want to go back and use it.'"

We found many other teachers who stayed happily in
teaching. Most of them met their multifaceted desires for
intellectual growth, challenge, and increased impact by
taking on new roles at their schools. Others, like Christine, entered graduate school to pursue intellectually challenging work, but plan to return to teaching later.
Attending to this facet of professional autonomy requires
careful deliberation and planning. We recommend you
think hard about your own needs for professional growth,
the unique contours of your situation, and the kinds of
professional opportunity available to you. Talk with your
mentors, contact local education organizations, and keep
a professional journal to record your ideas.

*What role does status-seeking play in your quest for au-
tonomy?* As we discuss throughout this book, teaching is
considered a low-status profession by many. It is also
considered noble, somewhat selfless work. (And there
are multiple sociohistorical reasons why altruism and
low status are correlated.) Geraldine Clifford and James
Guthrie (1988) wrote, "Society expects teachers to be
professionals but treats them like missionaries" (p. 30).
Society's treatment of teachers means that it is hard for
us to separate what parts of the desire for autonomy are
actually about autonomy (and what it inherently provides) and what parts are about society's judgment of
what it means to be a professional. Given U.S. society's
treatment of teachers and the frequent link between
autonomy—on the one hand—and increased status,
compensation, and recognition—on the other—it is
hard to disentangle the professional need for autonomy
from these other motivators for "moving up" some kind

of educator career ladder. Consider the number of former K–12 teachers who earn doctorates, find university faculty jobs in education departments, and retrospectively explain the shift in terms of having increased control over the content and daily schedule of their work.

How much of the autonomy equation is true, and how much is entwined with the harder-to-admit desire for the elevated status of professor over that of a school teacher? We do not discount the importance of status; it is real and linked to legitimate life-work satisfactions. However, we urge teachers to separate their own desire for professional autonomy from society's constant (and constantly flawed) belief that those who can, do, and those who can't, teach. Instead, we recommend you be honest with yourself. Consider what role status plays in your decisions, and why. Clarify for yourself what actual professional rewards and satisfactions derive from increased autonomy, and increased status, and predict what consequences they will afford you. Discuss this topic with others who have shifted out of classroom teaching: you may find that society's notions of status seem important at first but ultimately fade away. It may be the concrete characteristics of the work that ultimately matter.

Do you need to move away from the classroom to find freedom? Although "moving up" the educational hierarchy may seem a logical step for those seeking greater autonomy and impact, this movement up and away from the classroom may not be the most satisfying—as illustrated by Armando's experiences. Because there is a deeply embedded perception, on the part of many, of an upward trajectory where teachers become school administrators and then perhaps district officials or beyond, many talented teachers may feel subtle pressure to follow such a path. Following a less-traveled road, or paving a new one, however, may offer greater professional control and increased opportunities for effecting social change, and may ultimately prove more rewarding to the individuals who forge their own career paths.

Diana, for example, found ways to remain challenged and enact her professional autonomy without leaving teaching. In the next chapter you will meet other educators who found ways to stay connected and professionally challenged as classroom teachers.

DISCUSSION QUESTIONS

1. If you are just beginning your teaching career, what kind of autonomy do you expect you will need in order to be successful? (Picture what it will look like.) What circumstances might pull or push you out of the classroom?

2. If you are already teaching, do you believe you currently have sufficient autonomy as a teacher? If not, what are the factors that limit your professional autonomy, and what can you do to secure more autonomy for yourself as a teacher?

3. Is your work intellectually challenging? Do you experience an exciting, constant pressure to keep learning, to think hard and act well, and to be challenged to consider things in new ways? If not, how might you seek out learning challenges?

4. What role does status-seeking play in your quest for autonomy as an educator?

5. Do you think you will need to move away from the classroom to find increased autonomy? If so, why do you think this is?

FURTHER READING

Ayers, W. 1995. *To Become a Teacher: Making a Difference in Children's Lives.* New York: Teachers College Press.

Fessler, R., and J. Christensen, eds. 1992. *The Teacher Career Cycle: Understanding and Guiding the Professional Development of Teachers.* Boston: Allyn and Bacon.

Ingersoll, R. 2003. *Who Controls Teachers' Work? Power and Accountability in America's Schools.* Cambridge, MA: Harvard University Press.

CHAPTER THREE

BUILDING SOCIAL NETWORKS

OCIAL RELATIONSHIPS are an enormous part of educators' work lives. Often, we find job opportunities through our personal connections and seek advice from trusted friends, family members, and mentors—people who know us well. Before making career decisions, we consider the way our existing relationships will be affected, what we stand to gain or lose socially, and the interpersonal demands of a new job. We attempt to figure out whom we are likely to work alongside, to what degree the work itself will be collaborative, and to what extent we think we will fit in—based on various criteria like gender, personality, shared interests, backgrounds, political views, and values. Once we begin a job, relationships can influence whether and for how long we stay. Indeed, strong, positive relationships can function like a kind of social glue that holds us even in jobs we might otherwise leave for potentially greener professional pastures. On the flip side, the absence of strong relationships or the presence of negative, stress-inducing ones can drive us away from one job and toward another. In this chapter, you will meet three more educators whose career pathways illustrate the powerful role that social relationships and networks play in shaping our actions. First, however, we provide a brief overview of the history, structures, and culture that define the social networks of educators and their work lives.

FRAMING THE COMPLEXITY: WHAT ARE SOCIAL NETWORKS AND WHY ARE THEY IMPORTANT?

Historical Roots

This social dimension of careers in education and the decision-making process that helps shape these careers is well studied and has deep historical roots. From one-roomed schoolhouses to the comprehensive schooling structures that have dominated the landscape of American education since the early twentieth century, changes to public schooling have also meant changes in the way teaching has been regarded as a profession and enacted as a career. Whereas the nineteenth-century schoolhouse generally brought one teacher together with a small group of multiage students whom she would likely teach for the entirety of their formal schooling, newer social efficiency models consolidated small schools into larger ones, with departments, areas of specialization, and often many more students per teacher.

Despite bringing so many students and teachers together under one roof, these modern "egg-crate" organizational structures and resulting routines of practice emphasized efficiency over collaboration. Although so-called normal schools had existed in the United States since the early 1830s to prepare teachers for the job of teaching (thus supporting the idea that teaching requires specific knowledge), the dominant paradigm emphasized the need for teachers to learn with others *before* and *for* teaching rather than *during* and *from* teaching. As a result, the expectation and reality throughout the twentieth century was that teachers work largely in isolation from one another, behind the closed doors of their respective classrooms. (For more on the history of isolation in teaching, see Fullan and Hargreaves 1996; Herbst 1989.)

By the mid-1920s, single purpose normal schools and teachers colleges had largely disappeared in favor of teacher education programs embedded within state colleges and universities. In recent decades, pathways into teaching have proliferated, with the growing popularity of district-based teaching internships and organizations like Teach for America. In the midst of the debate about how best to prepare teachers for work with the nation's schoolchildren, various efforts have been made to articulate clearly what teachers need to know and do in order to demonstrate excellence and develop in their craft. As already mentioned in this book, various efforts to professionalize teaching and draw attention to teacher learning over the course of a career have taken hold.

At the same time, both the teaching profession and schools have been pressed to change in response to new knowledge about how people—students and teachers alike—learn. In particular, research has drawn attention to the situated nature of individual development and idea that learning occurs within specific social, cultural, and historical contexts. Sociocultural learning theory's concept of "communities of practice," for example, describes knowledge as diffuse and shared and learning as a product and process that occurs when individuals come together in social practices organized around shared goals, norms, and values (Wenger 1998). Since its development, this concept—among others—has influenced various domains of professional practice as businesses, schools, and other organizations seek to improve learning for both individuals and the collective. Likewise, research has highlighted the importance of relational trust as a measure of organizational health generally and in school change efforts especially (e.g., Bryk and Schneider 2002). Guided by these and other research findings, many education reform efforts of the past few decades have emphasized the need to reorganize schools in ways that privilege social relationships among educators and students.

Cross-Reference
For discussion of the role of culture in learning, see Book 2, Chapter 1.

Social Network Perspective

Focus point

Building on the idea that learning is social and situated, sociologists in the 1960s began actually mapping and quantifying social relationships—suggesting that we are all embedded in a variety of social networks that determine not only what and how we learn but a wider range of resources, including support, information, opportunities, and influence. Since then, the term "social network" has gained currency and been applied widely across various academic domains. Those who employ a social network perspective are concerned with the relations—or "ties"—between individuals and the resources—often called "social capital"—that these relationships provide. Researchers examine social networks everywhere, from inside ethnic communities to online chat rooms to corporations, and ask questions about what these webs of relationships provide for their group members and the collective groups.

To understand how much social network thinking has become a part of mainstream American culture, one has only to consider the well-known phrase *six degrees of separation,* coined after Stanley Milgram's "small world experiment" in which he found that random Americans could be connected to one another through an average of only six relations. Consider, too, the widely read book *The Tipping Point,* in which Malcolm Gladwell uncovers the role of social networks in facilitating the seemingly disproportionate impact of otherwise small events through the dissemination and proliferation of information. In it, he discusses—much like social network theorists—the different roles that individuals play in social phenomena depending upon their unique positions in the networks of which they are a part.

Social network theorists use a variety of tools to explain the nature, composition, and strength of our relationships to others. For example, many studies have shown that the "birds of a feather flock together" phenomenon (called *homophily*) occurs frequently in individuals' networks (McPherson, Smith-Lovin, and Cook 2001); in other words, research demonstrates empirically our tendency to associate with others who are similar to us in some way. Research has also explored how the strength of our "bonding ties," or relationships to others, determine the degree of network cohesion and trust that we experience and the degree to which our networks provide safe spaces that encourage the kind of risk-taking that often generates new knowledge (Argote 1999). Among teachers, these strong ties create the trust needed to open up one's practice, collaborate, admit struggles, and offer constructive criticism, all of which play a crucial role in school change and improvement. In addition to bonding ties, we also rely on *bridging ties* to diversify our networks and bring previously unconnected people or groups together (Gittell and Vidal 1998). *Network diversity*—or the degree of difference across ties and network members—is both an opportunity and outcome of cultivating relationships with new and different people who excite us, challenge us, and help us grow. These technical terms are tools that help researchers describe how educators are embedded in a variety of social networks that guide decisions about their work and careers.

Three Types of Networks

Educators are many things: employees in particular workplace contexts, professionals in a particular field, and otherwise situated social beings. *Based on our research with teachers in urban public schools, we identify three particularly important kinds of networks—school-based, professionwide, and personal-professional—for those currently considering or navigating careers in education.* The complexity of social embeddedness is such that we all are part of multiple and often overlapping networks. Teachers are no different. Those we profile, like all teachers, are embedded to varying degrees and in varying ways in school-based, professionwide, and personal networks—

Focus point

all of which have the capacity to powerfully influence the opportunities these teachers have and the decisions they make about their careers. Here we tell the stories of Emma, Frances, and Grace to highlight features of these three different and yet often overlapping networks.

STORIES

Emma: Building Strong and Diverse Networks to Change Schools

Having worked in the same elementary school for the past ten years, Emma is embedded in a strong school-based social network. When asked why she remains "really dedicated to this school," Emma was quick to list the supportive relationships present, as well as the school and community conditions that she believed helped to make those relationships possible. She cited the presence of an inspiring principal, "a real instructional leader," who provided opportunities for her to develop her areas of interest (for example, in science instruction), valued her expertise, and invited her to take on various teacher-leader roles. In part, Emma attributed her decision to stay in the school thus far to this supportive relationship and the opportunities it afforded:

> I have a principal who values my opinion. . . . I get to be involved in a lot of different things. . . . I always want something new and more challenging. . . . Being here definitely has allowed me to be content in teaching because I've had the opportunity for lots of other challenges.

In addition to her own teaching work, these challenges included serving as Gifted and Talented Education (GATE) coordinator, technology coordinator, writing coordinator, and lead science teacher. Emma was also a core member of the school's instructional leadership team for six years and worked closely with the principal for the past few summers analyzing data from district and state assessments and staff surveys, and planning schoolwide professional development. In this way, Emma developed strong, trusting ties with those "higher up" in the organizational structure of schools, who had the chance to see her expertise in action and who came to view her as a reliable professional. Proving her competence in these diverse and challenging contexts has shaped and advanced Emma's career in important ways.

In her eighth year teaching, at the encouragement of her principal, colleagues, and others in the local district, Emma entered a district-sponsored administrative credentialing program. Although she worried about her capacity to do an administrative job well, those around her—her network—were attempting to convince her otherwise.

> I'm not sure I would deal well with the bureaucracy. I'd get myself in trouble, because I have a real strong opinion about what we're here for—the kids. They should be the focus. . . . I'd be a principal that would be in the classroom every day. I think that's another reason why people keep encouraging me to become an administrator. That's their vision of what a good principal is and does.

Emma's many school-based professional experiences also positioned her for a number of formal leadership roles beyond the school site—thus threatening to pull Emma away from the strong school-based network she so valued. Similar to Armando, Emma is one of the many young, talented, energetic, early-career teachers who are "invited out" of the classroom by supportive administrators who recognize their skill as teachers and their potential as educational leaders. And like Armando, Emma has mixed feelings: "There are lots of people pressuring me . . . not pressuring me exactly, but encouraging me to go into administration because I'm interested in professional development and instruction."

Despite pulls away from it, Emma has stayed in the classroom and the school, in large part because of the sustaining and rewarding social relations—strong ties—among staff, students, and families. She felt the strength of these relationships was directly related to the school's small size and the relative low rate of transience in the community. As Emma explained:

> A lot of [teachers] have been there for their entire career, some have had the parents of their students, some even had the grandparents of the kids they have now. . . . The parents and community are so supportive of us as teachers.

She also felt that the smallness of her school allowed teachers to work together, build community, and develop enduring relationships with one another, students, and families. As she put it, "We know all the children; it's not a 'my kids' situation—they're all our students."

Beyond her work in the classroom and formal leadership capacities, Emma started an annual Family Math and Science Night and worked to bring an early college-awareness program to campus. She even earned a master's in psychology "on the side" in part because "there have been a lot of social-emotional issues with families and kids, and I felt it would assist me, not helping as a psychologist or anything, but in being able to provide people with the right referrals and resources." When asked about the impact of her work, Emma mentioned "differences that I make that are not educational," like helping connect families to low-cost health clinics or other resources that they might not otherwise know about. This, coupled with a record and reputation for rigor and success in the classroom, contributed to Emma's strong identity as a change-minded educator.

Not surprisingly, she felt she was "pretty instrumental" in bringing about positive change in her classroom and throughout the school and derived a huge sense of accomplishment from this work.

Emma's professional network is both strong and diverse. She has close ties to colleagues, many of whom are older and more experienced in teaching and life than she. Emma also benefits from her close ties, spanning age levels, to generations of the almost exclusively low-income Asian and Latino families. The strong and trusting relationships with her principal and local district leaders are influential in situating her in the local education hierarchy. Moreover, Emma enjoys a strong alumni network of young UCLA-educated teachers, graduates of her psychology master's program, and peers from her district-sponsored administrative credential program. Clearly, the strong ties that define these multiple, overlapping, and diverse networks provide Emma with a variety of resources, information, influence, and support—an array of social capital that is helping Emma shape her career in ways that promote equity and change.

INTERLUDE: A TALE OF TWO SCHOOL NETWORKS   We know that many, many teachers do not find such strong and fertile school-based networks, particularly in urban schools. In one of our previous studies, we explored the experiences of early career educators working in two different schools—one that resembled Emma's and one that shared little beyond similar student and community demographics. Like Emma's, the first school site experienced low turnover and had a staff of fully credentialed teachers with range of experience and expertise, including veteran educators who had taught in the school long term and newer staff members who were eager to engage the community in novel ways. At this school, there was a supportive teacher-led inquiry group in which roughly a dozen coworkers gathered regularly to share teaching advice, discuss research, and plan school improvement projects including school-wide family nights and after-school programs. Much like Emma's principal, the school leader actively supported both group and individual efforts to improve school culture. Relationships between school staff and families were strong and positive; families were a regular and welcome presence on school grounds and in actual classrooms, and teachers spoke of frequent invitations to family events—birthday parties, baby showers, and little league games. As a result, all four of the teachers we interviewed and observed at the school reported feelings of efficacy and attachment to their school community, and all were present at the school the following year. Like Emma, they attributed their retention to the school-based network, the social fabric or glue that defined its relationships.

The texture of the social fabric was quite different in the second school we studied. There, four similarly prepared early-career teachers reported general career dissatisfaction. They attributed this mostly to the administration's leadership style and the resulting school culture, which was marked by distrust among colleagues. They spoke of feeling "overworked and undercompensated," pressured to accept responsibilities for which they were not entirely ready. They expressed a desire for more guidance and mentorship, but high rates of teacher turnover had left behind few veteran teachers and many novices. As one third-year teacher explained,

> When you're a new teacher [at this school] and you're busting your ass, . . . there's no one to support you and show you how, or to give you that chance to grow. It's like sink or swim.

Rifts within the larger faculty led to clearly defined cliques and territoriality. Although these four teachers viewed one another as friends and allies, they worked at different grade levels and had limited opportunities to formally collaborate. All spoke of strong relationships with parents and community members but had the sense that their administrators and colleagues distrusted and discouraged these alliances. Despite dissatisfaction with the overall school culture, the teachers expressed a strong commitment to the families and children with whom they worked.

These teachers were embedded in a school-based network that included administrators they could not trust, few veteran teachers to whom they had little access, parents and families distanced by school culture, colleagues with whom they interacted little, and a bunch of equally inexperienced and overwhelmed early-career peers. This was hardly a web of relations likely to improve practice or mobilize school change. Instead, school-based relations seemed more likely to generate frustration and hopelessness, leading to a departure from the school or the profession. And indeed, this is what occurred: all but one had moved on to other school sites by the following fall. *Tragically, this form of attrition is common and can cement a sense of hopelessness at hard-to-teach schools. Educators who opt to stay and fight against the grain in such schools often find a foothold in particular departments or networks of change-minded teachers that help sustain their commitment to change. For some, these networks extend beyond their school to the broader profession of education.*

Focus point

Frances: Seeking Opportunities for Teachers to Be Heard

Like Emma, Frances has stayed closely connected to classroom teaching. At the time we spoke to her, she was eight years out of UCLA's Teacher Education Program, working as a National Board–certified middle school math teacher in Oakland, California; a teacher leader for the Bay Area Math Project; and a member of both the California and National Teacher Advisory Councils. As Frances talked about her identity as an educator, the importance of broad, professional networks as contexts for learning, identity development, and career development emerged.

Early in her career, Frances moved and changed jobs a few times, but always within education and always mindfully connecting with networks beyond the immediate context of traditionally bounded school or workplace communities. For example, during her first two years teaching at a Los Angeles public school, she made a concerted effort to stay connected to UCLA and its California Math Project. When changes in her personal life took her to northern California, she taught in a middle school for another year, and then moved to New York because her boyfriend was offered a job in what seemed like an exciting new place to live, even if temporarily. There, she took a position at a national for-profit student support organization, what she considered "a great opportunity" given that "for me, the choice to leave the classroom wasn't because I didn't want to teach. It was about logistics, practicality. I didn't want to sign onto something and then be in a position to leave midyear." In this sense, Frances's early career was perhaps not unlike those of other recent college graduates, who have the freedom to bounce around geographically, testing the waters in other cities or regions before deciding where to settle. Regardless, Frances's core commitment to teach math seemed to help her find and take advantage of opportunities that kept her meaningfully connected to that profession and specialization. And, although she may not have initially recognized it, working at the educational organization provided entrée into a nationwide organization that would ultimately offer Frances a degree of career stability despite a second major relocation.

When she decided to move back west, Frances leveraged the organization's national network to ease her cross-country transition, transferring into a slightly higher-status position in the organization's northern

California center. This new opportunity proved valuable in multiple ways. First, Frances imagined that it "felt the way it would feel to be administrator, because you're managing a business—all sides of it, working with students, management of other adults, doing sales with parents coming in, all those different aspects of a school, although it's definitely a business and not a school." Thus, she was able to do what many young people desire: explore the contours of a job without having to make a long-term commitment. Based in part on this experience, Frances told us that she never wanted to be an administrator.

Second, the Oakland job involved visiting her students' schools throughout the Bay Area and talking to teachers. As a result, she became familiar with many schools and built good social relationships with their staff. Through these connections—or bridging ties— Frances learned about an upcoming math vacancy and jumped at the chance to return to the classroom in a school she knew fairly well: the Marina Middle School. Whereas many new teachers only know well the few schools where they attended, student-taught, or had personal connections, Frances had the chance to explore an entire system of school communities. Her satisfaction at Marina, where she has taught for the past four years and plans to teach indefinitely, relates in part to her ability to make a well-informed decision at the outset about whether the school would be a good fit for her—a good school-based network.

During her first year back in the classroom, Frances immediately sought out the Bay Area branch of the California Math Project, the statewide organization with which Frances had been involved in Los Angeles and with which she wanted to reconnect, "because it was this important piece of my identity as a teacher." Since these subject matter projects are housed at UCLA alongside Frances's teacher education program, they had been

accessible from the start of her career. She also actively
sought out other professionwide networks focused on
what it means to be an accomplished professional in her
field. For example, she earned National Board certification in early adolescent mathematics; in an article in
2007, she describes this as "my single most profound professional development experience," and explains that she
now coaches other teachers through the certification process. The opportunity to be support provider for others
pursuing National Board certification proved meaningful
on both a personal and professional level since it gave
Frances the opportunity to work closely with teachers
who, like herself, were seeking to deepen their craft. Also
important for Frances, the compensation was "commensurate," as opposed to many other opportunities she had
been offered: "too many times they want a mentor
teacher to do something—a week in summer, prep time,
and follow-up, or something like that, for $1,000! It's not
reasonable."

**Teachers'
lives "are so
crowded and
hectic these
days that it
can be easy
to disregard
opportunities
to grow all
around us."**

Frances offers this advice to her colleagues: "There are
many opportunities for ambitious, passionate, gifted
mathematics and science teachers, but you must seek
them out." She counsels that teachers' lives "are so
crowded and hectic these days that it can be easy to disregard opportunities to grow all around us." Frances's
far-reaching networks—her alumni network, her
school-based network, her statewide content-based network, and the national professional network—also
opened the door to yet another opportunity: to serve as
one of twelve members on a first-ever statewide Teacher
Advisory Council, a group of California math and science teachers modeled on the national Teacher Advisory
Council. The group meets three times a year, and, as
Frances explains,

> I'm the youngest. It's mostly veteran teachers, and the
> goal is to really bring the teacher voice to education

policy. . . . [As a group, we're] nonpartisan, but we need a message, so we've done a lot with crafting our message. We have met with our assembly district representatives. We represent all of California, rural, urban, independent, public . . . and we're all highly accomplished teachers of math and science.

According to Frances, being chosen for the position "has everything to do with UCLA," specifically her relationship with a cherished and influential adviser who "put my name out there." Perhaps not surprisingly, Frances advises other teachers to seek out mentors who can influence their careers: "Do not underestimate the connections and relationships you make." This may seem an obvious statement, but in reality, it broaches a somewhat taboo topic in a profession whose members are often characterized as selfless and nurturing and rarely as ambitious, interested in career advancement, and desiring of professional recognition.

Though this high-status, professionwide work has great meaning for Frances, it never replaced her work "on the ground" with students in her classroom. On the contrary, Frances strongly expressed her belief that accomplished teachers need to be with students on a daily basis as well as become active members of broader networks. She describes this belief and her commitment to multiple professional roles rooted in classroom teaching as follows:

I am a teacher because I love learning and I am passionate about mathematics education. I enthusiastically bring my energy to the classroom where I believe that all students can be successful. . . . I do not believe that my career path as an educator must take me out of the classroom. I believe that there must be more opportunities for accomplished teachers to learn, grow, and have their voices heard, without leaving teaching.

POSSIBLE ROLE IN EDUCATION: POLICY ADVISER

Modeled after the National Teacher Advisory Council, the California Teacher Advisory Council (CalTAC) is composed of math and science teachers who serve as liaisons connecting the teaching, academic, and business communities throughout California (other states have similar councils). CalTAC teacher leaders disseminate public-policy information to classroom teachers and provide feedback from them to university and corporate leaders on issues concerning math and science instruction. For information, see http://www.ccst.us/ccstinfo/caltac.php.

Focus point

Frances's networks have enabled a career in which she can continue to teach while also engaging in the broader professional, political, and policy conversation about what it means to be an accomplished teacher, particularly in the areas of math and science. Yet Frances, like Emma, also touched upon the role of these networks in exerting subtle and not-so-subtle pushes and pulls away from her core commitment to classroom teaching. For example, she recounted how leaders of the California Math Project had offered to buy out her teaching contract so that she could take over a leadership position. Although she values and supports the group's work immensely, she declined, explaining, "It's not where I want my career to go, providing professional development to schools. I want to be in the classroom." Interestingly enough, offers like these only increased alongside her accomplishments as a classroom teacher, a phenomenon that has troubled Frances on a personal and professional level:

That's part of the whole system—how quickly the powers that be want to yank you out of the classroom once you become accomplished. The way I see it, if you're good at what you do, if you have passion, have energy, you should be with students.

Frances's core commitment—to teach and leverage the power and possibility of a professional teaching career— is one she has been able to meet through a patchwork of positions and responsibilities that are anchored to and orbit around the art and science of teaching math. "That's what we talk about at CalTAC, modeling *this*, this is what it is to be a professional in education, to seek out these opportunities. That means a lot to me, that's what my path has looked like—pushing, trying, setting goals, trying to keep reaching." And indeed, Frances's story highlights a prominent theme in this book: how one can have an impact at the level of individual students while also working more broadly toward a vision of educational change. Frances has found one answer to this challenging question in large part through her connections to and cultivation of professionwide networks.

Grace: Negotiating Balance Across Multiple Roles

Looking back over Grace's ten-year career illuminates how personal networks often overlap with professional ones, and how personal/professional balance is negotiated within and across a variety of social networks. When we spoke with Grace, her current position defied an easy title. She was working 80 percent time, spending half of that as a school administrator two days a week and half as a district employee in charge of teacher support. Despite the fact that she never intended a permanent departure from classroom teaching, she was generally happy with the variety and flexibility of her present situation. The path that brought her to this place has quite a lot to do with the interaction between her personal and professional networks.

Grace spent the first four years of her education career teaching multiage K–1–2 at a K–8 school in a relatively small district with strong connections to the UCLA Teacher Education Program, including an official partnership and numerous, well-known university-affiliated employees. Grace also had firsthand experience in this district since she worked there as a student teacher and was among a large number of UCLA teachers who were hired the following year. As a result, Grace began her teaching career alongside friends and fellow students, effectively importing an already formed network of professional colleagues. Indeed, this has long been an explicit goal of UCLA's Teacher Education Program and the reason it places at least two first-year (or "resident") teachers in any particular school site.

In contrast to the unfamiliar social terrain many teachers face upon entering their first teaching job, Grace walked into a supportive social network and was immediately invited to join an "inquiry group" where she and fellow alumni gathered to vent, collaborate, and wrestle collectively with what it meant to be equity-minded educators. Although she and three other fellow program graduates had been regularly meeting together in an informal support group, this inquiry group—whose members worked at schools across the district and who are still in regular contact now ten years later—met Grace's need "for a sense of collegiality, a safe circle, that's situational. You need to know the schools in a district. . . . We've always met and read and discussed. That group of us, it's the necessary sounding board." In this way, Grace echoes research findings about teachers' need for opportunities to engage with a regular community of like-minded peers (e.g., Nieto 2003; Lieberman and Miller 2001; Cochran-Smith and Lytle 1993, 1999).

Although she had no immediate plans to leave the classroom, at the start of her fifth year Grace was approached

POSSIBLE ROLE IN EDUCATION:
TEACHER SUPPORT PROVIDER

California's induction program for beginning teachers—called Beginning Teacher Support and Assessment (or BTSA)—provides formative assessment and individualized support to newly credentialed teachers. All teachers seeking a credential in California are required to successfully complete two years of BTSA participation. BTSA relies on experienced classroom teachers to supply mentorship and support. Other states have similar induction programs and mentoring opportunities for experienced teachers.

by the district and asked if she would be interested in helping establish the district's new Beginning Teacher Support and Assessment (BTSA) program.

She accepted the invitation and moved to the central office to work as a teacher on special assignment. She did this job for two years and then accepted a district position as coordinator of teacher support. A year later, Grace scaled this assignment back to 40 percent so she could take on an exciting new role as a part-time assistant principal. She explained:

> I had done my admin credential through the district [administrative credential partnership program with a local graduate university] part-time, and this job [coordinator of teacher support] kept getting other responsibilities. The piece about being an assistant principal just came up last year. I went to present findings on research on all-day kindergarten to the school board. The school board president said [this particular school] needed an AP. The principal and I were friends from [the administrative credential program], and it just sort of worked out.

Alongside these career moves in and out of schools, roles, and district offices, Grace was also pursuing a long-held dream to create a new progressive alternative small school in her district—a district in which she felt there was a need for "options for kids who don't thrive" in traditional settings.

POSSIBLE ROLE IN EDUCATION: SCHOOL DEVELOPER

Several national school reform organizations support educators who want to create new schools. The Big Picture Company (www.bigpicture.org) designs public schools and trains educators to "serve as leaders in their schools and communities, and actively engage the public as participants and decision makers." Other national school reform organizations devoted to developing new schools include the Coalition of Essential Schools and the School Redesign Network.

In this school development work, Grace also found opportunity and support in her social network, specifically in her longstanding friendship with a fellow graduate of UCLA's program who had also been working in various capacities in the district. Together the two, along with another friend, spent more than two years crafting a proposal to start a school that they believed would provide better conditions for teaching and learning. Grace and her friend were new mothers at the time and wrote a shared principalship into the proposal. She explained the personal-professional rationale for these choices:

> I don't want to be a full-time principal. I'm not willing to sacrifice my time with my toddler and [another child] if we have [one]. But to be a leader of a school with all the design pieces and ten years of proof behind the model, and people like Debbie Meier providing professional development on a nationwide model in a public

system with public money, each of us working three days
a week—that was the ideal.

The school proposal ultimately fell through for political reasons; however, along the way, the planning process
hooked Grace up with The Big Picture Company, a well-
known national school reform organization. Acting as a
bridge to the broader world of school transformation,
this connection provided Grace with a national forum to
share, and be recognized for, her innovative ideas.
Although the proposed new school never came to
fruition, Grace acknowledged positive outcomes of her
role as a bridge between the progressive organization and
the traditional school district: "I now see the School
Board initiating on their own to create some smaller high
schools in the district . . . so I see my work as having
influenced them to move in that direction." And since
part of the failed attempt to create a school involved
working with families and students to incorporate their
input into the proposal she presented to the district,
Grace's efforts had served as a bridge in that sense as
well, "communicating [to the district] the benefits of this
high school model, where the usual high school doesn't
allow for flexibility for kids. . . . All of these families were
talking about heading towards college and wanting real-
world experiences for their kids." Introducing this alternative vision of schooling was a powerful experience for
Grace.

The delicate and deliberate balance between personal
and professional priorities that Grace sought continued,
and it was something she mentioned repeatedly. For
example, when asked about the advice she—as a teacher
support expert in her district—would give new teachers;
she said there were many things she would advise and on
many different levels, but the following was central:

The California Standard for the Teaching Profession 6.6.
It's the one about personal-professional balance and

"I'm surrounded by really inspired and motivated teachers who run themselves ragged. The political passion and work ethic is there, but it's not tempered enough with the things that keep them physically well."

well-being, because I'm surrounded by really inspired and motivated teachers who run themselves ragged. The political passion and work ethic is there, but it's not tempered enough with the things that keep them physically well.

For Grace, a big part of well-being involved spending time with her family and being the kind of parent she envisioned. This appears to be a central concern of many teachers, especially during their midcareer phase—when they have professional clout and confidence and personally are becoming spouses and parents. Like others we interviewed, Grace acknowledged that jobs in education can be as big and time-consuming as one makes them. In addition to the already emotionally, intellectually and physically taxing work of teaching, school structures and eager administrators typically ask talented teachers to give as much or more than they can give in other ways as well. As a result, teachers who are not protective of their time and energy often run the risk of early career burnout.

Grace told us she plans to stay in education but was not sure in what capacity. The following year would be the first that she would not be working directly with teachers in their classrooms, and she expressed ambivalence about this loss of what she had earlier called "the best part of my job." Not easily confined by job titles, however, Grace expects that she may still "create opportunities to carve out opportunities to directly work with teachers, at least a little." Looking back on her career, Grace admitted, "I thought I'd go back to the classroom, but each year I'm funneled more toward [a focus on] my administrative credential than [on] my teaching credential." She acknowledged that there was a "subtle, or not so subtle, really, external pressure to move away from [the] classroom." Here, Grace echoes the comments of Armando, Emma, Frances, and many others who struggle with the following career tension: *How do I stay*

connected to the core work of teaching—directly facilitating
student learning—in a profession that rewards me for tak-
ing on roles and responsibilities beyond the classroom?

The stories profiled in this chapter all provide evidence of the mainstream expectation that accomplished
teachers eventually leave the classroom. And they also all
suggest that movement out of the classroom is as much
the product of one's social networks as it is the function
of any autonomous career decision. The professionals
whom we connect with while we teach—those people we
call our peers or mentors—have great and often hidden
influences on the shapes of our careers in education.

CONCLUSION: THOUGHTFULLY AND STRATEGICALLY BUILD POWERFUL SOCIAL NETWORKS

The first insight that emerges from these stories is both
trite and profound, commonly called for but less often
heeded: know yourself. Such an endeavor takes work and
is always unfinished, because we change with the accu-
mulation of life experience, in relation to changes around
us, and in connection with those we know and care
about. Still, deep self-reflection can help you better craft
a career that fits the life you think you want. Social networks are about choice and chance. Many things we cannot plan for—falling in love, losing a parent, having a
baby. Careers are somewhat easier to control. If you
know your personality, the kinds of autonomy you seek
in your work, and the resources—in time, wisdom, or
money—that you hope to have available for family and
friends in the future, you can thoughtfully and strategically build powerful social networks that will help get
you there.

As education researcher Ricardo Stanton-Salazar
(2001) explains, "An individual's *network orientation* constitutes an important dimension of human consciousness,
and can be understood as a rather complex constellation

of dispositions and skills related to network-building and adaptation to environmental demands, stressors, and opportunities" (p. 24). *Educators face particular environmental demands, stressors, and opportunities in their work. Accommodating instruction to the needs of many students, managing time well, taking care of oneself, working for change in institutional contexts organized to perpetuate the status quo, making decisions about careers—these are all areas in which our networks might assist us if we knew and were willing and able to find and make use of the advice, information, and influence they have to offer.*

Focus point

Emma, Frances, and Grace were all able to recognize, access, and effectively make use of the social capital to which they had access. They were "resource seeking" in the sense that they actively pursued connections and opportunities that they believed would improve their teaching and move their career forward. They all created a variety of diverse networks characterized by bonding and bridging ties. Yet we can imagine that not everyone would think and act the way these educators did, even if embedded in similar networks. Doing so requires being aware of the resources in your networks, confident about taking risks, and savvy in managing multiple and complex social relations.

These three educators' stories also suggest the importance of seeking out people who understand and share your core commitments. For those considering careers in education, this means looking carefully at entry routes and programs, because they have the potential to connect you (or not) to a community of like-minded peers. Many of the educators we studied shared the value of being "embedded" in alumni communities in the area where they all worked. Most everyone still claimed close relationships with either or both student and faculty members of UCLA's Teacher Education Program. Some, like Frances, spoke candidly about the role that these relationships played in securing opportunities later in her career.

Being intentional about where and with whom you choose to work also has major implications for the kind of work you will do and the degree to which that work will provide autonomy and social support. Who will you put yourself in contact with? Which networks will you join, thereby creating professional communities and affiliations that will equip you for your career? We recommend you attempt to predict where your core commitments will find a comfortable home and the degree to which sociostructural conditions will support you to fulfill those commitments. For those entering their first school site, we suggest talking candidly with families, teachers, and administrators at potential workplaces. In Emma's case, finding a fit was to a certain degree a mix of preparedness and luck. The school where she was first hired to work exceeded even her own expectations for what it would provide in terms of support and opportunity. For Frances, as we know, there was more strategy involved—more purposeful research into the kinds of networks that existed to support the kind of work she sought to do. And although her professionwide networks are the ones that seem to sustain her career most, the value of the school-based network they helped her to find is not to be underestimated. One need only to recall the experiences of Christine—detailed in Chapter 2—to remember the power of places where one is autonomous to the extreme of being isolated.

Still, we would not want this issue to sway teachers away from work in challenging contexts. Rather, we hope it encourages teachers to pay attention to the range of resources that a school community has to offer and to decide under what conditions one might be best able to fulfill one's core commitments in that context and whether and how one could work toward the creation of the conditions. For example, Christine described a "man against the machine" struggle; here, the problem may not be the struggle so much as the singular pronoun—framing the protagonist as an individual rather than a united group. People allied together have a better chance against the machine than does one lone hero. As the book's opening passage about Jaime Escalante suggests, the kind of change that equity-minded educators seek to effect often requires collective effort. Indeed, any look at the history of education reveals that, together, educators and communities have accomplished a great deal even in the most challenging of circumstances. Thus, for those working in schools, we emphasize the significant potential in breaking the bonds of privacy at and beyond the workplace and instead seeking out personal and professional experiences that connect you to others who share your passion for issues of educational justice.

DISCUSSION QUESTIONS

1. If you are currently teaching, what are your existing school-based, professionwide, and personal-professional networks? How will you thoughtfully and strategically build on these social networks to cultivate network diversity and move your career forward?

2. Have you been intentional about where and with whom you choose to work? Do your school and colleagues provide the support you need to be effective and nurtured? If not, how might you find a more supportive work environment? Where else could you look for your support network? If you are just beginning teaching, how will you locate and join effective support networks?

3. What professional networks or community organizations will you join to extend and deepen your career beyond the classroom and to build ties between your school and other groups in or beyond the local community?

FURTHER READING

Fullan, Michael, and Andrew Hargreaves. 1996. *What's Worth Fighting for in Your School.* New York: Teachers College Press.

Nieto, Sonia. 2003. *What Keeps Teachers Going?* New York: Teachers College Press.

Oakes, Jeannie, John Rogers, and Martin Lipton. 2006. *Learning Power: Organizing for Education and Justice.* New York: Teachers College Press.

CHAPTER FOUR

MAKING A DIFFERENCE

W E ALL CRAVE MEANING. As humans, we want our lives to make sense and have significance. We want to leave the world a better place. We want to make a difference. But what does it mean to leave the world different or better than you found it? What does it mean to live a life that is significant or meaningful? Philosophers have struggled with this vexing issue for centuries, and theories abound across disciplines to explain this unique feature of humanity. Anthropologists study the systems of meaning that are constructed in different cultures. Religious scholars ponder the meaning of human life in relation to God's will. Novelists invent characters who struggle to define their own significance. And neuroscientists argue that our brains are wired to search for coherence and meaning. In fact, our survival depends on it. So, in some sense, do our careers.

As the previous two chapters have illustrated, teachers' careers follow a variety of pathways, formed by the struggle for professional autonomy, status, and freedom and shaped by different types of social networks. A third struggle that determines career pathways is the *search for meaning and significance*. A heady struggle to be sure, the search for meaning starts with our core values and unique histories and extends into the world through the opportunities it creates. Along the way, each of us develops a coherent story about our career or life's work that defines our value in society and helps sustain us over time.

FRAMING THE COMPLEXITY: WHAT DOES IT MEAN TO MAKE A DIFFERENCE IN EDUCATION?

Countering the Legacy of Low Status

Like most professions, teaching has a strong tradition that defines its social value and significance. As we explained in Chapter 1, the educators we studied challenge this tradition of teaching as low-status childcare by instead framing it as powerful political and intellectual work. Several teachers we interviewed ran head-first into the dominant tradition as soon as they announced their decision to go into education to their families. One teacher explained her parents' reaction to the news:

> "You're so smart, why do you want to be a teacher? You could be a lawyer, a doctor, anything you want to be. So many other things make more money, why do you want to become a teacher?" And I said, "You know what? I just feel that." I gave them a reason why I didn't want to be a doctor and a lawyer, and I said I just feel that with teaching I'm going to be interacting with people and making a difference, and that's really what I want to do.

As this teacher explained to her parents, there is an alternative value system—making a difference—that helps collectively define the search for meaning among the educators we studied. In turn, this value system helps assign a higher social status to the work, both within and outside the profession of education. The proliferation of career labels symbolizes this higher-status frame. *Teacher* is variously replaced by *educational activist, change agent, teacher-scholar, social justice educator, public intellectual, instructional leader, educator for social responsibility, urban educator*, and so on. These career labels are status markers within our society—they signal heightened power, prestige, and value. And as we have seen, these labels often signify careers that take teachers out of the classroom to increase their impact or significance. Throughout this book we have used the label *change-minded educator* because it signifies a core career tension—working within a system and trying to change it at the same time. This label, however, doesn't capture the types of change or reform or difference these educators are seeking. To communicate the focus of their efforts, we have often called them *equity-minded educators*. It is time now, however, to situate these broad labels in a historical context to understand the collective beliefs, values, and expectations that undergird the tradition of educators actively working to make a difference.

Members of an Activist Tradition

In contrast to the female-dominated tradition of compliant teachers, the change-minded educators we studied belong to a tradition of activists—from social reformers, to members of religious communities, to legal advocates, to revolutionaries—who fight against society's many forms of oppression and inequality. As graduates of UCLA's Teacher Education Program, they each participated in a community that valued this activist tradition and placed them in Los Angeles's most challenging urban schools. As students, they were encouraged to claim "the role of educators as well as activists based on political consciousness and on ideological commitment to diminishing the inequities of American life" (Cochran Smith 1998, p. 116). They were encouraged to imagine themselves as part of the broader community of educators—Fannie Lou Hamer, Jane Addams, Myles Horton, Chico Mendes— who have historically struggled for social justice and not settled for the ways things are (Hunt 1998, p. xiii). As

Cross-Reference
See Book 5, Chapter 3, for discussion of social justice teaching and community building.

Focus point

Kenneth Zeichner (1993, 14) sums up this core value, "The most important point is that teaching cannot be neutral." *Activist educators are expected to take a stand and to fight for what they believe. When they engage in the fight, they experience the power of participating in a collective cultural struggle, which in turn shapes their identity as powerful and significant individuals.*

POLITICAL WORK IN TEACHING/EDUCATION: THE HIGHLANDER CENTER

In 1932, Myles Horton helped found Highlander, a center devoted to democratic leadership, grassroots organizing, and transformative social change. During the civil rights movement in particular, Highlander played an important role as a gathering place for leaders like Rosa Parks and established Citizenship Schools to help spread literacy and voter education. Today, Highlander continues to offer workshops, internships, and programs for those committed to social justice and equity. For information see www.highlandercenter.org.

Changing Schools and Systems

"Schools embody the dreams we have for our children."

To be sure, teaching is not neutral; it is always an act guided by a vision of what the world *should* look like. As small schools pioneer Deborah Meier (1995, p. 11) puts it, "Schools embody the dreams we have for our children." Similarly, each educator is guided by a vision of schooling that directs his or her activism—the changes they each seek and value. For some, schools are sites for creating possible worlds guided by democratic, multicultural, and egalitarian values. They believe that social inequality is sustained by a set of practices and values that divide people along lines of race, class, gender, and other salient social categories. Working to change these practices means constructing learning environments where students, teachers, and parents experience a microcosm of an alternative social life—democratic spaces that value student voice, multiculturalism, and creativity.

For others, schools are impersonal factorylike structures that impede learning and run counter to the human need for significance. Their vision of what could be is rooted in theories of learning and humane organizations. They fight against bureaucratic schools that aim to pour specialized units of knowledge into the heads of passive consumers and then measure their success according to regurgitation rates on standardized tests, administered at regulated intervals. Working to change these practices means developing challenging and engaging student-centered classrooms where success is measured authentically by what students know and are able to do.

Still other educators are motivated by a larger vision of an educational system that promotes equity and excellence across schools. This might mean working to redistribute educational goods such as access to Advanced Placement courses or good teachers that have historically been concentrated in privileged communities. It might also mean advocating for policies that heighten professional practice—as opposed to teacher-proof mandates—thereby elevating the quality of teaching and learning for all students. Activist educators work in all of these ways and more to change schools and the larger system.

Educators gauge their ability to make changes in schools and systems in a number of ways. Many look for evidence. Some teachers see their impact firsthand in assessments of their students' growth throughout the day, month, or year. Others look to school graduation rates or former students' college pathways and reason that they have played a role in these successes. And those working beyond the classroom witness their impact in policies they helped create, teachers they helped retain, schools they helped build, or any number of other measurable achievements. Each of these forms of evidence and many more are used to explain how educators help achieve educational equity or level the playing field. For many people, these are ways to prove to themselves and others that they are indeed making a difference.

Connecting with Students

In addition to the expectation that activist educators take a stand and change schools and systems, a third set of values expresses a hallmark commitment of all educators—the importance of connecting with students and relating to their lives. This is a core value that extends across time and traditions. For many, many educators, their connections to students define their work. They show up each day to touch lives. They find the work of teaching simply a joy. Each day, they experience the meaning of their work in their connection to students. Some experience a similar quality of relationship with parents as well. At some point in their career, most educators struggle to achieve this quality of experience because the conditions of their work or their life preclude strong relationships, encourage cynicism, or overwhelm their ability to connect with students. This is when teachers burn out, their human drive to connect with others extinguished. When this happens, the work of teaching can seem meaningless. Conversely, the experience of connecting with a student—seeing that lightbulb go off or inspiring the spark of motivation to succeed—is perhaps the foundational definition of how and why teachers make a difference.

Focus point

These three sets of core values—taking a stand, changing schools and systems, and connecting with students—capture important dimensions of how change-minded educators frame the meaning and significance of their work, how they make a difference. There are, of course, many more dimensions; this is complex terrain. By foregrounding these three sets of values we hope to rein in the enormous question of how and why the life's work of a change-minded educator has meaning. Each set of values suggests a corresponding set of expectations, and we turn back now to our seven educators in order to witness their struggles to meet these challenging expectations and find meaning in their work.

Each of the seven educators has a unique history and set of reasons for becoming activist educators. For Armando, it was firsthand experience of racial injustice and the drive to address social inequalities through education. For Diana, it was growing up amid gang violence in Los Angeles and experiencing an assault that grounded her conviction in the power of education to change lives and society. For Barbara, it was outrage at the discrimination leveled at Spanish-speaking students. For each person, there are many reasons to enter education and participate in its activist tradition; we do not presume to capture them all. Instead, our goal in this chapter is to understand how these educators struggle to make a difference by meeting the core expectations of their profession as they travel along their career pathways.

STORIES

Armando: A Fight to Be Fought

As part of a broader tradition of activists, Armando intended a career as a civil rights lawyer but, after graduating from law school and taking the bar, he decided against pursuing a career as an attorney. Early on, interning with different civil rights organizations, he found the profession to be "unscrupulous" and too stressful. As detailed in Chapter 2, Armando taught for three and a half years and then was "tapped on the shoulder" to become a school administrator. In both of these roles, Armando has found meaning in "the fight"; he explains, "You never know where the fight is going to come from, but the fight is always to do what is best for social justice, to help kids." By engaging in the fight, Armando explains his struggle to make a difference:

> For a lot of students, really like myself . . . the only way in which they're going to find any semblance of equality in this culture, financially or socially, is through an education. And that's what I see myself fighting for all the time. Sometimes that fight is with fellow administrators who might have a sort of deficit model of thinking of students. Sometimes that fight is with certain teachers who also feel that way, that our students come in with a deficit. Sometimes that fight is with certain parents, who feel that their children should have preferences for certain classes over the others. Sometimes that fight is with community members. I mean, you just never know where that fight is going to come from.

One of the reasons Armando stays in education is that he worries that others will not fight the fight; as he explains, "I'm afraid that if I walk away, who will [fight]? You know, who will stand up for this Spanish-speaking single mother who continually tells me that the teacher hangs up on her?" Armando experiences this worry as a powerful motivation to stay put.

As an administrator, Armando believes he is better positioned for this fight than he was in the classroom because he is aware of schoolwide issues and can use his position to influence policy changes:

> You tend to be aware of a lot more things schoolwide. And because of that and the position that you have where you can influence people, sometimes if you use your position to influence policy change or maybe even influence district-level administrators about things that need to change, I think that I'm definitely in a better position to do that than if I was just a teacher.

Yet, Armando's first experience effecting schoolwide change was as a teacher. Responding to the low school morale surrounding him as a third-year teacher, Armando organized a group of teachers who met in his classroom to take positive action. What started as a "vent session" progressed quickly, due in part to the support of the principal. Armando explains the evolution of the group:

> We started thinking about things, collaborating on things, agreeing on things; there was automatic buy-in from the teachers because we were developing a lot of things that we could do, such as, OK, who is going to monitor the hallways, there's always kids running around. Who is going to do this, who's going to do that? What about grades? What are we going to do if a kid is not doing well? What type of support network? Just a lot of things that came up. And so I started seeing that it really had an impact schoolwide, and I thought to myself, "Wow, this is good, this is something that I can see myself doing, and so, how do I do this?" Even though I'm impacting a school on a schoolwide basis I still feel limited because I'm in here in a classroom teaching. If I had more time I could probably impact it more.

The changes Armando refers to are school-level practices, structures, and policies that support student learning and the work of teachers. Coming together to take action together was a powerful experience because it resulted in concrete schoolwide changes. As Armando said, he could *see* that it really had an impact.

When he moved from the classroom into the role of an assistant principal, in hopes of making more of an impact or difference, Armando described the experience as a roller coaster, where the search for meaning was tied to stress, work hours, the time of the year, and so on. Once again, he describes "the fight":

It's always a fight to be fought. Sometimes you don't
have the energy to fight it, so you choose another battle,
but when you do have energy and you recharge your
battery you feel that it is worth continuing to fight. And
that's the way that I feel right now. I feel optimistic and
that it is worth continuing to fight. But when I'm run
down and I'm working here till twelve, one in the morn-
ing, then you start questioning whether it is worth it or
not. . . . It's a roller coaster. . . . You have times where
you believe that you truly do impact the school. And at
other times where you really doubt yourself.

Part of the doubt surrounding his ability to make a difference stemmed from the nature of school bureaucracies, the seemingly futile school reform mill, and the
difficulty of gaining traction given the high attrition rates
that plague urban schools. Armando explained that
teachers who don't want change just wait out the
inevitable change in administrative guard. The doubt
also stemmed from his lack of teaching experience. As
detailed earlier, Armando felt that he left the classroom
too early. Now, as an administrator, he confesses to feeling like an imposter at times. He explained that he sometimes confides in others about this insecurity, and they
respond, "What are you talking about? You're making a
difference." But Armando's not sure; as he puts it, "I
don't know. I just feel like it's not up to my standards."

Pressed to articulate what matters most in his search
for meaning, Armando talks about his relationships with
students, parents, and community members. Working
within a racially mixed neighborhood and school,
Armando feels that he is able to connect with one group
in particular:

After talking to parents and students I feel as if they feel
very welcome to the school as a result of the fact that I'm
here, either because of my mannerisms, either because I
speak Spanish, either because they can identify with my

background having grown up in the neighborhood, graduating from here, having come up, grown up poor, I don't know, but I just feel like there's a connection there with a large segment of the community, and I think they look to me to provide a voice for their concerns, as I do lead one of the parent groups here. That's what gives me meaning.

This human connection, rooted in shared identity and common experience, is a powerful reason to stay. Armando reflects on his own ability to connect with others, his interpersonal skills, and his capacity for empathy as ways that he makes a difference. In particular, he experiences this difference when he relates to students: "I always feel like I hit a home run in that area, and that to me is very satisfying. A lot of kids will tell me, 'You really understand what I'm going through and what the experience is.'"

Christine: Woman Against the Machine

Like Armando, Christine left the classroom to find a bigger stage for fighting against educational inequity. Along the way, they both entered graduate school because it seemed like a logical professional step. As Armando progressed in his doctoral program, he confessed that he didn't think it was improving his ability to lead in any way. Instead, he thought the experience was giving him specialized knowledge in a narrow area and that this knowledge would make him more aware of particular issues. "Honestly," he said, he entered the doctoral program because he "didn't know what he wanted to do." In contrast, Christine's decision was quite deliberate. She describes herself as "very philosophical; I enjoy ideas, and I will probably do some work in philosophies of policies, like what's the underlying goal and what's the underlying assumption. That will be part of my work, I'm sure—but ultimately, what's most fulfilling is when I can go into schools and work with people." These two pursuits, intellectual and working in schools with people, define Christine's search for meaning in education.

Throughout her three teaching placements (see Chapter 2), Christine struggled to figure out how to fight the system—as she put it, "man against the machine." In doing so, she seemed to take a sociological stance, recognizing that she was fighting against "a huge environment and a set of relationships that are far older and more ingrained than you, and that reproduce themselves and the system in the social reproduction sense." With her move to the charter school, she finally gained autonomy, though with little support, and felt that she had influenced the lives of her students tremendously; yet she experienced much tension about her ability to affect the system:

> As a practitioner, working with kids who were disengaged, I realized that there were institutional factors that created their disengagement. I needed to try to maintain a systemic perspective of their disengagement, not a personal, individualistic one. At the same time, I could only help those kids if I dealt with them as individuals, and one part of my role was to help them develop personal responsibility. This was a constant tension—knowing that I'm working within a system that as a system perpetuates disengagement, but I as an individual have this personal relationship with this student who has some agency. Together, we could use our agency to diverge to a degree from the institutional norms. I felt that there was a chance that I could reach that student in a way that "the system" was not encouraging.

As a teacher in a self-contained middle school classroom with "high-risk" adolescents, Christine tried to reconcile this tension by providing traditional class structures and practices such as homework, star charts, and daily assessments—"things that in a regular room count." She described her classroom as "highly regulated

and predictable," governed by the teacher as the author-
ity figure. Christine was acutely aware of the problems
and tensions that her approach suggested, admitting that
"it sounds so controlling and behaviorist and supportive
of the institution that socializes them to be good little
workers, and I feel that tension constantly." Nonetheless,
she believed "that was the best way that I could do a service with these kids." This approach to teaching gave
Christine immediate measures of her impact on students.
Every day, she sent home a daily report with students
that detailed their work and achievements. She explained
the report's value:

> It was a way for parents to be aware and to be proud and
> for the kid to self-regulate and see progress. I had to be
> incredibly consistent, because this group needed that . . .
> and when the kid makes these changes from red to
> green, that's progress and it's public and recognized. I
> never used it for shaming. That's something I really
> worked hard on and had to learn. I had to learn how to
> make it all positive, as positive as possible, as often as
> possible.

Christine used these reports to help guide and keep track
of students' progress—along the way they served as a tool
to help her assess the value and impact of her teaching.

Despite the "substantial change in the lives of students" she witnessed in her classroom, Christine
remained plagued by problems endemic to the system or
machine: "I invested considerably in my individual relationships with kids, but the tension was to prepare them
to go back to regular schools. In the system. The system
that perpetuates the disengagement." This tension was
too great, prompting her decision to enter a Ph.D. program in education:

> Coming back to graduate school was a way to address
> institutional forces, the larger system. When I say that,

I don't necessarily mean public education in the U.S.,
and I certainly don't mean public education in the
world at large, western schooling, although I used to
think that. Now I'm more interested in if I can work
with community-day schools or a network of middle
schools. That's where it's at for me, because I could
make some systemic impact and still work with kids.

What Christine seems to be grappling with is finding a
context for making systemic change that is close to students. Like most teachers, Christine experienced enormous reward through her relationships with students.
Her main challenge is to find a hospitable context for
redirecting the machine that allows her to fight alongside and on behalf of students. When asked about how
she is making a difference, Christine admits that her
search for meaning is still unresolved and the project to
gauge the impact of her work is enormously complex
and multifaceted.

Frances: Think Globally, Teach Locally

In contrast to the uncertainty and tension embedded in
Christine's career path and search for meaning, Frances's
quest is grounded firmly in the classroom, supported by
a constellation of professional associations (see Chapter
3). Like Christine, Frances seeks to make a systemic difference, but she is confident the best way to do this is by
teaching math. Frances is vehement that her voice be
heard while remaining as a classroom teacher: "The way
I see it, if you're good at what you do, if you have passion, have energy, you should be with students." The role
of teacher provides a platform upon which Frances cred-
ibly fights for larger educational issues. She has sought
out and fallen into a variety of teacher leadership opportunities that have allowed her to take a stand. As she
explains, these opportunities are instrumental in defining
her professional significance:

My experience in CalTAC has been profound. It gives me the opportunity to rise above the daily challenges of teaching and look globally at the ways education and policy are related, to share my voice about the reality of what is going on in my classroom every day, and to feel valued as a professional outside the classroom.

Frances strongly identifies with the growing tradition of teacher professionalism. Her activism is grounded in the belief that those who work closest to students are best positioned to understand and make change within the system. As part of this tradition, Frances also believes strongly in the value of the National Board for Professional Teaching Standards (NBPTS) and its vision of what counts as accomplished teaching. In reaction to the long history of disrespect for teaching—the belief that anyone can teach—the NBPTS has articulated a clear set of standards according to which teachers can measure or gauge their own mastery.

These standards are a compelling framework to capture how teachers make a difference in the lives of students. For example, National Board–certified teachers

PROFESSIONALIZATION WORK IN TEACHING/EDUCATION: NATIONAL BOARD FOR PROFESSIONAL TEACHING STANDARDS (NBPTS)

Founded in 1987, the NBPTS establishes advanced proficiency standards and certifies teachers meeting those standards. Experienced teachers interested in obtaining certification must prepare a professional portfolio, record their classroom practices, and pass a written exam. NBPTS standards are closely linked to national teacher preparation standards, and many states and school districts offer tangible financial incentives, such as salary increases, to National Board–certified teachers. For more information visit http://www.nbpts.org.

are expected to "critically examine their practice on a regular basis to deepen knowledge, expand their repertoire of skills, and incorporate new findings into their practice." In doing so, teachers like Frances are constantly evaluating their success with students and learning how to improve their craft. Recall from Chapter 3 all the opportunities Frances creates for her own professional growth; as she said, "I create experiences to keep learning." These experiences are core to Frances's search for meaning in her career.

Asked to articulate how she gauges the impact of her work, Frances talked about creating a classroom where mathematics is not feared:

> The huge thing for me, my main goal as classroom teacher, is my relationships with students. . . . In the content area of math, there is such negativity about the subject, about doing it, about self-concept, and then there's the reality, like Thomas Friedman's *The World is Flat* . . . the idea that we're doing a poor job educating students in math and science. I love the fact that my enthusiasm and my relationships with students can color their experience of math in positive ways, and I can see that from students saying and showing that they're not afraid of math, that they embrace it and enjoy it. . . . I have this girl, for example, who says, "I don't want to go to my next class, can I stay in here?" Another girl I tutor has really struggled with learning disabilities, really struggled. We have built this solid relationship. We meet 2–3 times a week, and she's doing it—she's taking Algebra 2 in the summer. It's not her strength, but we have fun, we laugh. We talk about determinants and matrices, but we also connect.

Frances's ability to create a possible world where mathematics comes alive through strong, solid relationships with students is what keeps her going. She knows she is making a difference each day and week as she engages directly with students and experiences their growth. This, for Frances, is what it means to make a difference.

Emma: Planting Seeds

Emma is also a National Board–certified teacher, and, like Frances, she is always looking for opportunities to learn more and improve her craft. As detailed in Chapter 3, Emma has taken on a number of professional development responsibilities beyond her classroom, earned a graduate degree in psychology, and enrolled in a leadership training program—all to expand her repertoire of skills and incorporate new strategies into her teaching practice. She also shares Frances's core commitment to the centrality of classroom teaching:

> I just feel like once you move out of the classroom, you lose touch. As a teacher, it's hard to take directives from people who have been out of the classroom for 10–15 years. Things change, students change, schools change, programs change. If you're going to be someone who makes decisions about the daily lives of kids, you need to understand what those kids and teachers deal with every day.

Emma's own professional significance and status is rooted in the quality of her teaching practice. The fight Emma fights is over instruction—making sure it meets the needs of her students and presses them to succeed. For example, she explained how she brings in supplementary materials when the mandated texts don't align with her philosophy. "My math," Emma described, "is a lot more Marilyn Burns than Harcourt Brace." Similarly, she explains how she is willing to push on scripted curriculum packages such as the Open Court reading program, saying, "I'm not going to move on if my students aren't ready for it," despite a strong districtwide push for uniform compliance. Asked about her own level of freedom to deviate from the mandated programs, she explained, "It depends on who the Open Court coach is for the year. If they decide they want me to do it, I either do it or I get written up. I have to decide if it's worth it."

When asked how she gauges her impact, Emma also appealed to evidence of students' progress:

> I'm very into analyzing data, and so as far as my students' achievement is concerned, I take a look at where they are when I get them, where they are when they leave me, and where they are along the way. To be honest, if they're not making progress, it really gets to me. So I spend a lot of time in the morning and afternoon doing intervention in order to make sure they're moving along.

Emma's reliance on measurable achievement gains has great appeal to many, as evidenced by the No Child Left Behind (NCLB) Act and its prescribed emphasis on standardized testing and adequate yearly progress. Although many educators have criticized the NCLB Act as overly narrow, discriminatory, and punitive, few would argue with the value of clear and measurable expectations for students. The profession of education provides a range of tools for measuring teachers' impact on students. In response to the NCLB Act's battery of tests and rubrics for gauging progress at various levels of the system, professional associations of educators have supported multiple forms of assessment, including performance-based measures and more authentic exhibitions of student mastery. The authenticity of these measures—the fact that they highlight students' "real world" achievements—often translates into heightened satisfaction for teachers.

Emma, like other elementary teachers, teaches the same group of children all day, which enables her to develop strong relationships with individual students and

ASSESSMENT WORK IN TEACHING/EDUCATION: THE NEW YORK PERFORMANCE STANDARDS CONSORTIUM

The consortium is a coalition of high schools nationally recognized for excellence that have pioneered the value and rigor of performance-based assessment tasks as alternatives to high-stakes testing. Tasks require students to demonstrate accomplishment in areas such as analytic thinking, research and writing, and the arts, and are evaluated by experts external to the schools. Consortium educators are committed to creating assessment systems that enhance, rather than compromise, student learning. For more information visit www.performanceassessment.org.

keep track of multiple assessments of their progress. Yet, probed about the difference they make in the lives of these children, many elementary teachers look to their students' futures as young adults. As Emma explains,

> This job is a hard one, but the kids are why I stay. It makes it all worth it when they come back and thank me, or a parent says, "You've made such a difference in my child's life." Them coming back and telling me really means a lot. I e-mail with former students, write letters, get visits from old students. My first class just found out whether they got into college, so a lot are coming in to say "I'm going to Pasadena City College," "I'm going to Long Beach State"; a couple are going to UCLA. I know that for most of these kids, they got to my class and they didn't know what college was. I know I planted the seed.

"This job is a hard one, but the kids are why I stay."

Emma's gardening metaphor is apt. She knows that her work with students is part of a much larger cycle or project—the development of a human being. What's interesting is the drive to define or pinpoint where teachers and teaching fit into this cycle. Whether it's planting a seed about college, teaching a child to read, or raising a test score, the expectations teachers like Emma set for themselves help them gauge their success and define their value.

Grace: Guided by a Big Picture

Grace's career is all over the map and defies easy description, but it is guided by a coherent educational vision. As detailed in the previous chapter, she moved from the classroom to the district office and then back to the school site as an administrator. Along the way, Grace worked very hard for two years to establish a new small school that would embody her educational dreams, including a coprincipalship that would define her future career. In fighting to create this small school "with all the design pieces and ten years of proof behind the model," as part of the national network of Big Picture schools, Grace was taking action against the traditional system of high schooling that depersonalizes learning and alienates both students and teachers. In this system, high school teachers see 150–200 students each day and measure their progress in Carnegie units earned, grade points accumulated, and high-stakes tests passed. In Grace's school, teacher "advisors" would stay with the same small group of students throughout high school, helping them define their own personalized learning plans and guiding them through a series of internships and learning experiences over four years. When students graduate from Big Picture schools—like the one Grace envisioned—their teachers experience great satisfaction in understanding and witnessing the impact they have had on students' lives. Referring to her school development partner, Grace explained, "It could have been exactly what we both wanted and believed in. We were close." Although the effort to start her own school was unsuccessful, she was proud that her work helped move the district toward exploring the creation of new small high schools. Some are being developed at present.

Guided by her progressive vision of schooling, Grace's work supporting teachers also gave her satisfaction. Although her current role as an assistant principal allows her to influence schoolwide culture and provides many opportunities to relate to teachers, students, and parents, Grace's role working directly with teachers and supporting their practice was particularly meaningful:

> Up through last year, I was working directly with teachers. I was in classrooms on school sites. It's really fulfilling personally, and you aren't guessing. You get the true deal, you get the frontline feedback on the work you're doing and the professional development you provide. And I'd be directly reporting that information to people on senior cabinet. I was given incredible leeway to implement anything, anything right for teachers in classrooms, because I'm collecting all this firsthand data and it's compelling and no one is going to argue with it.

Grace witnessed firsthand that "the experience [we provide] definitely does something that helps [teachers] feel connected to each other and empowered in their community and in their jobs" and also saw proof of positive impact in district studies of BTSA graduates who are retained at higher rates, come into leadership roles, pursue National Board certification, and return to the program as support providers. Moving away from her one-on-one coaching with teachers was disappointing to Grace, who confessed that in her new role, "I'm not sure my input will mean as much." Grace's case highlights the connection between professional fulfillment or significance and a clear understanding of one's impact. As she put it, it's when "you aren't guessing" about the value of your work that it makes the most sense and has meaning. Looking to the future, Grace hedges about the possibility of becoming a principal unless the school reflects her educational vision: "It has to be a school that I believe in heart and soul, or else it's working too hard for something that's just not worth it, just not what I'd completely believe in."

Barbara: Moving Outside the Box

Barbara also has a strong vision of the changes she seeks: "to help other Latinos not feel that just because they only spoke Spanish that they couldn't learn." Like Armando, Barbara identifies with her students and their struggles with language and culture. And, as we detailed in Chapter 2, Barbara was pulled out of the classroom because she thought she could make more of a difference. She was frustrated that teachers—especially teachers like her who advocated for Latino concerns and taught English-language learners—were not being heard within school reform and education policy circles. She tells the following story about attending a district meeting where they announced to a room full of teachers that a new writing assessment would be introduced the very next month:

> When I went to the meeting, three, four people said something, and there were probably 150 other people that were just like, "OK, whatever, it doesn't affect me, I don't care." So who cares if it's unjust? And that's the kind of attitude you get, and it's just like, I'm hoping that by being a principal, that I can be more of an advocate for my students. Or even a VP, maybe by being there for somebody else, and saying, "Look, you know what? You need to take a stand, or you need to do this, just rule, we'll be able to make more change." And then even creating that environment for teachers where they do feel comfortable and have that open relationship with their colleagues.

As Barbara summed up her career decision, "I feel that by going up, I'm going to have more of a voice than as a teacher." This voice was especially crucial, Barbara felt, with the increasingly compliance-oriented nature of teaching. "Creativity," she bemoaned, "is being shut down. And, basically, these assessments [presume] that the teachers must be idiots—that we need scripts to tell us what to do. Then people complain that teachers aren't motivated?! Well, why would you want to do what they tell you to do when they don't treat you like a professional?" Barbara framed her fight on behalf of both students and teachers.

Working within a supportive school, Barbara reported that "honestly, I love teaching first grade. I am so happy, teaching-wise I've never been happier." She felt that she was teaching her students important life lessons, such as how to be confident and strong. Like Frances and Emma, she also pursued many avenues for professional development that enhanced her teaching and impact on learning. In this pursuit and her rejection of scripted curriculum, Barbara expresses the importance and value of classroom teaching. Interestingly, however, this set of values seemed to clash with the logic that guided Barbara's decision to leave the classroom. She earned her administrative credential in order to "take that extra step." Many factors contributed to Barbara's decision to leave the classroom and follow this logic in search of a bigger impact, among them status, salary, and flexibility. In this way, her vision of the profession stands in stark contrast with Frances's and Emma's commitment to classroom teaching. In fact, Barbara indicated some disdain for career teachers:

> I don't want to be those teachers. There's one teacher here who has been here for twenty years. I'm like, "Lady, OK, I know you love kids and everything, but isn't there something else?" I mean, for me, when I first started teaching even, being in [the Teacher Education Program], I was like, yeah, I want to be this agent of change, but it can't be boxed in a teacher. I ought to go outside of that box and see how else I can change, so

when, you know, I take my hat off to teachers who stay in the profession for twenty, thirty years but you know, I'm like, what else have you done?

The expectation among change agents like Barbara is that they must leave the classroom to find other, perhaps more effective, ways to improve schooling and equalize patterns of school achievement. Whether or not Barbara's career adventure outside of the classroom box will prove more meaningful than teaching remains to be seen.

Diana: She's Still Here

Diana grew up not far from the urban school where she now teaches. During her first year student teaching, she was robbed at gunpoint—a terrifying incident that clarified what she calls "a mission to help children see the range of possibilities for their lives so that they don't see crime or this type of behavior as their only option." After teaching kindergarten in the same classroom, in the same school, for ten years, Diana frames the difference she has made in terms of the relationships she has established within her community:

> I've had a relationship with the same community, with the same kids who now have their brother and their two little sisters who have gone through my class, and I'm connected to the family. I feel like the students who have gone through my class, my presence at that school as they go on up to fifth grade or fourth grade, just my presence there says something to them in terms of my level of commitment: "Look, she's still here. A lot of teachers have left, a lot of my teachers that I've had, but I can always count on Miss D to be there; her door is always open; I can go in and help her." And I just feel like the consistency is important, and the kids see that people are committed to them and committed to being there for them.

Diana is striving to create a stable, nurturing school within her community that students and families can count on. Her ability to contribute to this possible world helps keep her going and defines her fight against society's neglect of the children and families she serves. As she explained early in her career, "I'm too angry to leave."

As detailed in Chapter 2, Diana created many opportunities for her own growth and advancement as a teacher, such as her sabbatical with the IDEA parent project. These were guided by her commitment to educational justice and a need to be a parent to her own children. Working alongside parents gave Diana enormous satisfaction, and she actively sought out ways to improve parents' relationship to schooling, including creating a Parent Center at her school site. Acknowledging that "a lot of times parents get blamed for every single thing," she felt empathetic toward the parents of her students and believed that parenthood has made her a "more powerful teacher."

In addition to the strong connection Diana experienced with fellow parents, she explained her impact on

PARTNERSHIP WORK IN TEACHING/EDUCATION: PARENT U-TURN

Parent U-turn, based in southeast Los Angeles, is a grassroots, multiracial parent advocacy group that supports low-income, first-generation, and immigrant families to better navigate public schools. Members work to improve the educational opportunities of urban students in the local community and partner with various education programs to inform teachers about families' rights and needs. For information on local parent groups like Parent U-turn, contact the Public Education Network (www.publiceducation.org) or the National Coalition for Parent Involvement in Education (www.ncpie.org).

students. Her kindergarten students are "a wonderfully rewarding age group to work with because you just see these massive growth gains from day one to the day you graduate them." Being able to witness a student's growth over the course of a year and know that you contributed to this growth is one of the hallmark rewards of teaching—defining for many what it means to make a difference. In addition, Diana articulates her connection to students:

> I just enjoy the children. . . . I've had kindergarten all these years. So you can't get more honest than that, you can't get a clearer perspective on life than through the eyes of a kindergartner, you know, they cut through all the fancy talk and just tell it like it is. . . . Being with the kids, and just, I don't know, it may sound esoteric or whatever, I get joy out of it. It is a preferred activity, if you will, for me to do.

"You can't get a clearer perspective on life than through the eyes of a kindergartner."

Even though Diana articulates the impact of her work on students and parents, she appeals in the end to the immediate quality of experience—the intrinsic reward in the here and now, not relative to some future goal or expectation. Though she expects and hopes the world to be a better place if good teachers stay committed to communities over the long haul, her fire to keep on going is fueled by her everyday experience working alongside five-year-olds.

CONCLUSION: WHAT IS THE BEST WAY TO MAKE YOUR DIFFERENCE?

As we have discussed in this chapter, there are three sets of core values that help define meaning and significance for activist educators: the value of taking a stand; the value of changing schools and systems; and the value of connecting with students and families. Each of these values maps onto a set of career expectations that are used to gauge the extent to which someone is making a difference. We have shared stories of seven powerful educators who struggle to make sense of their worth and value in these ways. As we've explained, *there are many ways these educators understand the impact of their work on the larger project to achieve equity through schooling. They witness it firsthand in assessments of their students' growth throughout the year. They hear first- or secondhand reports of former students who have achieved success, such as college admission. They see their schools change to become more responsive to teachers and students. And they experience the foundational value of connecting with their students and families, each day and over time.* These experiences and others help educators define their work as meaningful and significant.

Focus point

Each of the change-minded educators we studied is unique, yet they all share a common experience working in extremely challenging contexts: high-poverty urban schools that have historically reproduced social inequality. As we've seen, their efforts to change these schools and the larger educational system take them in many different career directions. We must acknowledge, however, that any of these pathways can be enormously stressful and can threaten to derail the careers of the most committed educators. As Grace explained, "I'm surrounded by really inspired and motivated teachers who run themselves ragged. The political passion and work ethic is there, but it's not tempered enough with the things that keep them physically well." Frances elaborates:

Cross-Reference
For more on archiving social justice and equity, see Book 4, Chapter 6.

> The drain that teaching is on yourself—especially in high needs and urban teaching—it's so big, the burnout. I had a really, really bad year this year. I never came so close to feeling what it might feel like to burn out. And it was my eighth year teaching! If I felt this the first year, I probably wouldn't be in teaching. How do you nurture yourself? It's so important. Especially teaching older kids, you absorb so many different feelings, emotions, personal problems from kids all day . . . what that does

all day, it builds up, it's hard. You can't let yourself burn
out, or you'll be a negative teacher, a horrible partner,
not a good friend to others in your life.

Not letting yourself burn out: this is perhaps the most
vexing project of all. Frances and Grace both suggest
that teachers must nurture themselves and take care of
their health. But as we've suggested throughout this
chapter, part of the project involves setting clear expectations for yourself based on a set of core values. Figure
out where you want to put your passion and energy
and why.

   "People go in all kinds of different directions,"
explains Christine. "I was with some really high-quality
peers, really passionate people; they're making a difference wherever they are." Diana explains career choices
she has seen her friends make: they decide to either "eke
out [a] little comfortable place in this messed-up system
and not make waves, or . . . make waves and get an ulcer,
or . . . move to some place where things happen." As the
saying goes, you have to pick your battles. Being strategic
about your career means in part figuring out what gives
you the most satisfaction. At the end of the day, what do
you consider a meaningful contribution to education
and society? Emma warns that it's really easy to lose sight
of your core beliefs once you're stuck in a large district or
institution. She advises teachers to "hold strong, to re-
read your mission statement, re-read some of the things
you learned about, revisit social justice and the idea of
evening the playing field . . . [and] stay true to your core
beliefs." Along with this good advice, we would add,
think hard about the expectations that go along with
these beliefs. Changing the world through education is a
tall order. Figuring out what it means to you will help
you find and create career opportunities that allow you
to make *your* difference.

DISCUSSION QUESTIONS

1. What are your own beliefs and values about how the work of educators is significant or makes a difference?

2. How do you consider, assess, or measure the impact of your own work in making a difference in the world?

3. To what extent do the conditions of your current work—your role, workplace, colleagues, etc.—inspire or dampen your core commitments and ability to make a difference? How might you improve upon these conditions?

4. If you are just beginning teaching, how will you intentionally seek out a position and/or school site that matches your own core commitments?

FURTHER READING

Hargreaves, Andy, and Michael Fullan. 2008. *Change Wars*. Bloomington, IN: Solution Tree.

Meier, Deborah. 1995. *The Power of Their Ideas: Lessons for America from a Small School in Harlem*. Boston: Beacon Press.

Rose, M. 1995. *Possible Lives: The Promise of Public Education in America*. New York: Penguin.

CHAPTER FIVE

THE DREAM JOB

- A New Vision of the Teaching Career
- Time, Money, and Opportunities
- Autonomy, Networks, and Meaning
- A Final Chorus

I

F SCHOOLS EMBODY the dreams we have for our children, then they should be run by professionals we trust to keep the dream alive. Yet, how often does society ask teachers about their dreams for making this happen—the type of work they think will best help students learn and grow? Throughout this book, you have heard the voices of accomplished educators struggling to construct careers that allow them to do this work well. Change-minded in their work, each has sought out multiple and overlapping opportunities to reform and improve schools while remaining connected to students. Their voices—and the changing face of the education profession—offer an inspiring view of what careers in education should look like. Although there is no one dream job, they suggest an ideal that we can all aspire to. In this closing chapter, we look back at the landscape of careers in education, this time focusing on the current research and advocacy work to change the profession—to reinvent teaching careers. We end by returning to the voices of our seven educators and their hopes for the future.

A NEW VISION OF THE TEACHING CAREER

More than a decade ago, noted teacher educator and scholar Linda Darling-Hammond (1997, p. 327) put forth the following recommendation:

> A new vision of the teaching career is needed that rewards the knowledge and expertise of those who work closest to children as highly as the skills of those who work furthest away and that makes those skills more widely available, thus enabling teachers to take on complementary hyphenated roles as school and program leaders, curriculum developers, mentors, staff developers, teacher educators, and researchers while they remain teachers.

This vision has gained momentum in several professional communities. For example, Ann Harman, the director of research for the National Board for Professional Teaching Standards, recommends creating new leadership roles for teachers, facilitated by flexible administrative structures that allow teachers to take on new roles, such as pre-service mentor, professional development coordinator, or university instructor, without leaving the classroom entirely. The Teacher Leaders Network represents another national community dedicated to supporting teachers' growth and development in research and advocacy roles that extend beyond the classroom but don't strip teachers of their core identity and work as educators. Throughout this book we have described a local professional community, UCLA's Teacher Education Program, that has also supported the vision of teachers as active and powerful intellectuals working to change Los Angeles urban schools through transformative teaching and learning. And there are many, many others doing similar work to reenvision teaching as a career that is rooted in, but also extends beyond, the classroom's four walls.

PROFESSIONAL DEVELOPMENT OPPORTUNITY: NETWORKS OF EDUCATIONAL LEADERS

The Teacher Leaders Network (TLN), a project of the Center for Teaching Quality, is a nationwide network of accomplished teacher leaders who are dedicated to student success and the transformation of teaching into a true profession. TLN operates an online forum where teacher leaders engage in discussions of policy and practice, collaborate on action research, share content and pedagogical expertise, and generate policy recommendations based on the wisdom of experienced educators. See www.teacherleaders.org.

Even teachers' unions have advocated for a fresh look at long-standing career and advancement structures; union activists in various cities are working to reenvision what it means to support teachers and their profession. Union-developed and/or -approved career ladder initiatives, under way in cities like Rochester, New York, are establishing more flexible structures that allow teachers to have it all—career advancement tied to their core work as teachers. Under such initiatives, advancement does not require leaving the classroom. In Rochester, for example, lead teachers are selected by a joint panel of teachers and administrators; they take on leadership roles such as mentor, staff developer, and curriculum specialist but continue their accomplished teaching at least half time. In return, they earn additional compensation— potentially as much or more than local administrators. The goal is a system that rewards accomplished teacher leadership on par with accomplished school and district leadership, creates opportunities for experienced educators to mentor beginning teachers, provides incentives for excellent teachers to stay in the profession, and encourages learning and retention among teachers all along the career continuum. As Adam Urbanski and Carl O'Connell (2003, p. 7) explain, this staffing framework provides "an opportunity for exemplary teachers to inspire excellence in the profession, share their knowledge and expertise with others, and actively participate in instructional decision making *without* leaving."

PROFESSIONAL ADVANCEMENT OPPORTUNITY: CAREER LADDER INITIATIVES

Rochester, New York's, Career in Teaching (CIT) program designates four stages—intern, resident teacher, professional teacher, and lead teacher—to a teacher's career and provides professional supports at each level. These include opportunities for highly accomplished teachers to share their skills through mentoring and peer review processes and to receive appropriate compensation for this valuable work. The National Commission on Teaching and America's Future (NCTAF) offers more information about these and other initiatives intended to establish teaching as a professionally rewarding career. For more information, visit www.nctaf.org.

The change-minded educators we studied offer another glimpse at the power and promise of what Darling-Hammond calls "complementary hyphenated roles." Perhaps the most vocal proponent for this vision, Frances is firmly rooted in her math classroom as well as several professional communities that enable her to advance her craft and play a powerful role in educational policy development. Emma too has stayed close to teaching and professionally active, although she struggles with the common tension that runs throughout this book: *How do you continue to stay in the classroom and directly impact children while at the same time taking on additional professional roles that pull you away from them?*

Working to resolve this tension—what many educators experience as competing demands—requires a complex balancing act. Seeking balance was a pursuit that resonated with all of the educators we studied. Some, like Frances and Diana, felt that they had found a productive balance, but others remained, to varying degrees, torn and uncertain. Grace is hoping that her future administrative work connects her to teachers, but she's not sure that will happen. Christine hopes to return to the classroom in some capacity after graduate school, but much remains up in the air. Armando has serious misgivings about his career pathway, as its "administrivia" has moved him away from students.

These experienced tensions highlight an important dimension of the dream job ideal. *If the profession is moving toward hybrid roles for teachers, how can the profession ensure these roles are complementary and not competing? How, in other words, does the work of teacher-plus-mentor, policy adviser, curriculum developer, and so on become a coherent, balanced whole—not a frenetic and overburdened work schedule?* To answer this question, we turn to three essential elements of the dream job.

Focus point

NUTS AND BOLTS: TIME, MONEY, AND OPPORTUNITIES

As is the case for many teachers, the educators we interviewed asserted unequivocally that they became teachers because they wanted to positively influence the lives of children and make the world a better place. A decade later, their core commitments have not changed. However, the inherent difficulties and structural constraints accompanying their goals are far clearer than they were before entering the classroom. As we have discussed throughout this book, each individual faces personal and professional challenges that accompany his or her aspirations, pushing and pulling educators from role to role and workplace to workplace. We have discussed how the struggle for professional autonomy, supportive networks, and meaningful impact has shaped these career pathways. Before turning back to these themes, let's consider a few nuts and bolts that define all careers—time, money, and opportunities.

Time

Everyone we interviewed talked about the pressures of time. Whether it was having enough personal time for themselves and their families, finding a way to balance their current workload while furthering their education, or simply carving out enough hours in the day to meets the demands of their jobs, working within the constraints of a twenty-four-hour day presents a very real challenge. Seeking to make a broader impact on their schools and the school system, the change-minded educators we studied had myriad professional responsibilities—teacher, leader, advocate, mentor, student, scholar, and on and on the list goes. Some might consider them models of the new vision of a teaching career. To varying degrees, however, they all struggled to find the time to do it all.

Now layer on the added complication that as we age, we usually take on another set of roles and responsibilities—spouse, parent, homeowner, caregiver. As individuals' professional lives progress through career cycles, resulting in expanded and varied roles, so too do their personal lives shift through life stages. With each stage come additional responsibilities, challenges, and joys, filling already full lives and placing even greater demands on their time. For some, this time crunch seriously compromises their quality of life; as Armando explains:

> I think [my job] also affects my wife. We don't have kids. My wife is finishing up with school, too. If we had kids, I don't think I could have this job, honestly. But it does impact my family in that my wife and I really can't spend time together. I'm always tired. . . . As a result of

that I get grouchy a lot when I'm tired; . . . during the school year it really impacts my quality of life because I find I'm not as happy. I never rest. . . . I gained a lot of weight because you never exercise, and you're always eating standing up or running. You don't get lunch. Stress and lack of exercise just, you know, it gets to you. It really does. And so it does affect my quality of life.

Inevitably, not having enough hours in the day to meet personal and professional obligations means something will give, and the educators we interviewed lamented the fact that a lack of time meant they often felt they could not do all their work and family life asked of them.

So what's the solution to this perennial and widespread problem? Hybrid careers—defined as complementary multiple roles—in education have several meanings, but in terms of time, the vision suggests that teachers take on multiple roles either simultaneously or sequentially. Many of the teachers we studied did it all, at the same time. Frances was at once teacher, policy adviser, and mentor, layering on responsibilities beyond the classroom using structures such as release time, summer vacation, and probably evenings and weekends. Or recall Grace's plan to develop a half-time coprincipalship to realize her dream of running a progressive school while raising children. Diana, in contrast, took time away from teaching for her sabbatical and then returned to apply what she had learned about parent engagement. We urge the profession to explore more structures for using time in ways that facilitate hybrid roles that are enacted simultaneously or sequentially. Otherwise, "teacher plus" will most certainly lead to teacher burnout.

Money

Adequate compensation is an additional concern for many educators. Comparatively low teacher salaries often force individuals to decide between their commitment to their work and their ability to adequately provide for themselves and their families. For some, this leads to undertaking additional or entirely different roles in search of more money. As in most professions, there is undoubtedly a "minimum threshold" required to be able to remain in the profession, but this threshold varies depending upon the individual factors at play at any particular time. For many prospective teachers, relatively high starting salaries and the white-collar work of teaching provide a means of upward social mobility. For others, the financial stability and security that come with tenure means they can focus on their own practice without the worry of competing for pay raises. Although most teachers enter the profession at a relatively young age, as their age increases so too do their familial obligations and desires—having a family, caring for aging parents, buying a house, planning for retirement—and their need for greater earnings. Many former classroom teachers, like Armando, would prefer to remain in the classroom if it were financially feasible. Unfortunately, teachers are not currently rewarded for staying in the classroom; the traditional hierarchy of the profession offers more money the further away one is from children.

Some have suggested "merit pay" or pay for performance as a way of increasing individual teacher salaries and allowing individuals to be recognized for a job well done. A type of market-based incentive structure, merit pay structures have spurred or accompanied educational reform initiatives across the country for the past 100 years. Proponents of merit pay argue that this objective compensation structure raises the bar of professionalism, encouraging accountability, decentralizing governance, and rewarding teachers for excellence—a paradigm shift sure to attract talented and motivated individuals to the profession. Rochester's Career in Teaching program is one example that seeks to reward teachers for hybrid careers based on their mastery as mentors and instructional leaders. Merit pay detractors counter that it is unfair, impractical, and divisive and ignores the underlying systemic problems pushing teachers out of the profession. Whether merit pay is the answer to low teacher salaries, comments by the educators in our study indicate that a restructuring of the current pay system is needed to keep teachers teaching.

Adequate compensation—"getting paid what we're worth"—is a concern for these educators, yet the conventional "stay for pay" wisdom rings hollow. Earning more is desirable, but they didn't enter the profession looking to strike it rich and their primary motivators to stay in or leave the classroom are not financial. Nonetheless, the current salary structure for educators who are actively pursuing avenues for making change across the system—including their classrooms—does very little to encourage creative hybrid careers. We support efforts within the profession to critically examine and change current salary structures to both reward and retain accomplished change-minded teachers in the classroom while allowing them to contribute their wisdom and expertise to change policy and practice throughout the educational system.

Opportunities

Hybrid teaching careers also depend on significant and meaningful opportunities for growth and contribution. Throughout this book we have chronicled the wealth of opportunities created and sought out by the highly educated and accomplished individuals we studied. This quest for growth is not atypical for teachers after their first few years of teaching, when the challenge to survive the classroom transitions into a quest to master it. For Emma and Frances, earning National Board certification provided a way to reflect upon and hone their pedagogical skills. For Diana, a sabbatical from teaching to focus on the Parent Project allowed her to "stretch" her thinking about education and her own teaching practices before returning to the classroom. For Barbara, the search for challenge and growth was met through earning a master's degree and taking on advocacy roles while remaining in the classroom. Each was able to ward off feelings of stagnation by taking advantage of meaningful learning opportunities and making use of multiple roles in teaching instead of leaving the classroom altogether.

For others, the pursuit of intellectual challenges took them away from the classroom. Armando, for example, sought professional stimulation in an administrative role. When speaking about his shift away from teaching, Armando said that for him teaching, while rewarding, had become frustrating—that he sometimes felt "like a hamster on a wheel"—and he was eager to make an impact beyond his classroom to the entire school and community. Returning to some of the benefits of his position as a school administrator, Armando told us, "I need to grow; I need to learn. I just have an insatiable appetite to learn, and whenever a job becomes stagnant I think about leaving. I'm growing here. I'm learning something new every day. That's the part I love." Finding ways to satisfy the multifaceted cravings for intellectual growth and challenge these opportunities are essential to the professional well-being and success of educators.

All too often, however, professional development opportunities are structured to impede—not inspire— learning. Witness the prevalence of the after-school in-service or workshop where learning is packaged by the outside consultant, who then delivers the district's message to an audience of tired teachers. Recall Barbara's frustration at being preached at regarding scripted curriculum. Unfortunately, this is the norm for learning opportunities within our educational system. Notice too that the educators we profiled were able to counter these norms. Diana's careful reading of her contract led to her year-long sustained inquiry about parent engagement. Grace's networks within her district and alumni circle led her to affiliate with a national reform organization that supported and mentored her attempt to open a new school. Christine couldn't find the time for reflection within the current system and left for graduate school so she could deeply engage in ideas concerning equity and school reform. None of these educators settled for packaged staff development opportunities. And some, like Barbara, actively railed against them. In so doing, these educators model an essential feature of the dream job—meaningful opportunities for intellectual engagement and growth.

The nuts and bolts of time, money, and opportunities help frame the dream job's structure. Yet the foundation of an ideal career lies in the three themes we have explored throughout this book. We briefly revisit these themes now in relation to the dream job ideal.

REVISITING THE FOUNDATION: AUTONOMY, NETWORKS, AND MEANING

The dream job is one that allows educators sufficient professional autonomy, embeds them in a variety of supportive social networks, and enables them to make a difference across many dimensions of the educational system—all while living a life that is happy and balanced. Throughout this book we have explained how the history, structure, and culture of schooling shape and often impede educators' struggles to achieve this ideal. We have also profiled impressive and creative acts by individuals who have navigated and often fought the system in order to construct jobs that allow them to flourish. We now reflect on what their experiences suggest for the field of education.

Focus point

Professional Autonomy

As discussed in Chapter 2, the pursuit of professional autonomy is a motivating factor in teachers' decisions to stay in or leave the classroom. Educators need, deserve, and thrive on freedom to exercise their professional judgment on behalf of students. Whether the educators profiled in this book climbed the hierarchical ladder into administration, followed a more circuitous route out of the classroom, or figured out a way to stay rooted in teaching, they all worked hard to create opportunities for professional autonomy in their work life. These individuals fought to exercise professional discretion and control with regard to curriculum development and implementation, professional advancement, and the policies and practices governing their work and, by extension, their students' success. In so doing, they often experienced enormous satisfaction and reward—demonstrating how their heightened autonomy was related to their retention in education.

What this means for the field of education is clear. Educational structures need to be created and maintained that foster professional autonomy within the classroom. Highly qualified teachers should be rewarded for utilizing their talents and knowledge, not controlled through scripted curricula and top-down mandates. Constraining professional freedom pushes good teachers out of the classroom. Instead of heeding the call for increased teacher accountability for student achievement in ways that limit professional autonomy, policymakers should explore more avenues for alternative assessments and school-based accountability structures. Just as each student is a unique individual with unique needs, so too are their teachers uniquely positioned to attend to those needs. Though we recognize that instructional prescriptions and scripts may be helpful to underqualified or inexperienced teachers, well-prepared, highly qualified professionals rarely benefit from having their expertise constrained. Rather than teaching from assigned texts, for example, teachers might be given the freedom to choose their own, or a combination, that would best fit their interests and talents while meeting educational goals and standards. Regardless of how autonomy is structured in the workplace, teaching professionals, properly qualified and certified to educate young people using research-based teaching and learning strategies, require opportunities to flourish—not be stifled by the educational system

Constraining professional freedom pushes good teachers out of the classroom.

and its long legacy of disrespect for teachers. Clearly, the dream job is one that allows educators the freedom and responsibility to exercise their powerful judgment in the best interest of children. This is, after all, what we have prepared and entrusted them to do.

Social Networks

Proper support networks, both professional and personal, make up another part of the dream. As we discussed in Chapter 3, teachers are embedded—to varying degrees and in varying ways—in school-based, professionwide, and personal-professional networks, all of which have the capacity to powerfully influence the opportunities they have and the decisions they make about their careers. Emma, Frances, and Grace, to different degrees, were all able to recognize, access, and effectively make use of their diverse networks to secure the social capital they needed to enact change. These social networks did not suddenly appear but developed over time and out of various accidental and deliberate circumstances, creating scaffolded opportunities for transformation. The teachers profiled here also attended a teacher education program that deliberately connected itself with educational and action researchers, professional development programs, and community organizers and activists so as to create meaningful opportunities for its graduates to continually grow and develop.

Within teacher education programs, professional associations, schools, district programs, community-based organizations, and other institutional structures that bring educators together, more attention needs to be paid to the power of social networks and the mobilization of social capital to effect change. *In Chapter 3, we advised educators to be intentional about where and with whom they choose to work because their networks will shape the nature, quality, and impact of their work. Similarly, educational institutions must be intentional about setting up networks or*

Focus point

professional learning communities for educators to both improve their practice and ensure their retention. And beyond education, community-based and activist networks must bring more educators into the fold in order to realize their common goal of transforming schools, particularly in high-poverty communities that face an array of challenges. In short, creating powerful social networks for educational change is a dream that must be shared by many.

Making a Difference

The quest for meaning is a complex one, driven by an individual's sense of purpose and core commitments.

The book's final theme, the search for meaning and significance, is perhaps the most crucial, and the most elusive, piece of the dream job puzzle. The dream job would be nothing if its professional autonomy and supportive networks did not result in work that was meaningful—that made a difference in the lives of children. Yet, as we explored in Chapter 4, the quest for meaning is a complex one, driven by an individual's sense of purpose and core commitments. Complicating this meaning-making process is the fact that it is often not enough to simply believe we are making a difference; we also want to measure our success. And in education, measuring success is a politically charged and complex task. Whereas the teachers we profiled were certainly articulate about their impact on students, they framed the meaning of their work in broader terms. Making a difference meant taking a stand, working to change schools and systems, and connecting with students and families.

What can the profession learn from these reform-minded educators? To begin with, we suggest providing space and support for the conversation. What counts as making a difference is too often left to the accountability pundits who measure the worth of education—and by association teachers—through test scores and other narrow measures. Expanding the national dialogue about what constitutes meaningful teaching and learning would help educators articulate the value of their work and attend to this vital dimension of their career satisfaction. At the local level, we also suggest that schools and districts provide support for reform-minded teachers who are seeking to make a difference both within and beyond their classrooms. Help them set clear, meaningful, and ambitious expectations for themselves and reward their success at every turn.

A FINAL CHORUS

Admittedly, the seven educators profiled in this book are atypical of the majority of teachers nationwide. Graduates of a specialized, urban-focused credentialing and master's program, these are highly qualified individuals who have chosen to teach in the high-poverty, low-performing schools eschewed by most others. Nationally, only 3 percent of similarly prepared beginning teachers work in high-poverty schools, and fewer than 6 percent of all education graduates express a desire for inner-city placements (Lyons 2007; National Partnership for Excellence and Accountability in Teaching 2000). Two of the seven teachers profiled have received national honors for their teaching excellence. Moreover, their personal characteristics also set them apart from teachers nationwide. Upon entering the workforce, nearly 85 percent of similarly educated teachers—those with a teaching credential and a master's degree—are white; only one-third of UCLA Teacher Education Program graduates fall into this racial category. In addition, many of these educators not only graduated from select universities but also grew up in the same types of communities in which they teach. Diana and Armando, for example, are teachers of color with advanced degrees working in the same neighborhood, and even same school, that they themselves attended.

Although unique, the educators we studied have faced struggles familiar to teachers everywhere. Their stories offer insight into the personal and professional trajectories we all continually construct over time. As we have seen, career decisions are rarely straightforward but instead derive from personal and professional equations made in complex contexts without accurate predictions about the future. For example, Armando's ascendance up the educational ladder from classroom teacher to school site administrator to, potentially, district-level supervisor charts a straight hierarchical course. But its origins—from a working-class Latino neighborhood to civil rights law to a social justice–focused teacher education program—are anything but common. For Diana, a seemingly horizontal trajectory as classroom teacher masks the subtle contours of her personal and professional pursuits as a wife, mother, inquiry group leader, journalist, university instructor, parent-project leader, and community activist—and undersells her power as a successful educator working directly with children, their families, and the community. After listening to these educators tell their professional tales and deconstructing how personal and professional factors influence their decisions to remain in or leave the classroom, perhaps the most important question has yet to be asked: How would they construct their dream job?

Reading their stories, it is not surprising that though they all envision unique pathways for themselves, each aspires to have a hybrid job—a combination of roles and responsibilities inside and outside the classroom—that would allow them first and foremost to make an impact in the lives of students. As a doctoral student, Christine is searching for a way to change the system, a desire closely aligned with her reason for pursuing teaching in the first place. Reflecting on her reasons for entering the profession, she states: "I went to UCLA because I wanted to change the world. I know it sounds naïve. It was naïve. I was naïve, but I was passionate, and still am passionate; now I just have a different set of information." Removed from the classroom, her dream of wanting "to be involved with teachers and kids in classrooms" remains. Regardless of her future title, Christine's dream job allows her to work "one-on-one with students and teachers."

Grace envisions her dream job similarly. Lamenting the distance from students and teachers accompanying her district roles, she says she misses the "one-on-one interaction." In a recent follow-up with Grace, she announced with much excitement that she might have found her dream job—an "ideal new principalship" at the alternative school where she did her student teaching more than a decade ago. Working alongside the outgoing principal, Grace currently spends four days a week at the school and one full day at home with her two preschoolers. Invigorated by this opportunity to enact her progressive education ideals while balancing her home life, Grace says she has a fifteen-year vision for the school and looks forward to having her own two boys attend as students.

For Barbara, the dream job combines the professional freedom and respect that exist outside the classroom with the ability to directly impact children inside the classroom. What would keep her in the classroom would be a dynamic and stimulating job, one with time for collaboration with colleagues and individual interaction with students. "I would love it," she says, "if we could meet once a month for a day, or have at least two hours a week . . . to be able to sit down and say, 'OK, what are we going to do for this upcoming month?' You know, what's going to be our theme, what's going to be our unit, how are we going to do it?" If she does leave the classroom, as is her current plan, she admits that she would "miss the kids" and "the whole one-on-one interaction" but is confident that she would find ways to "be in the classroom every day." Ultimately, she believes, this is what all educators envision: "It's not so much we're here for the paycheck. We're [all] here for the kids, what's good for the kids. Not what's good for us. It's like, what's good for our students, for their learning, and that's our top priority."

For Frances, students are similarly a top priority. As she continues her work in the classroom, she cites as her "main goal" to foster and maintain relationships with students. It is this aspect of her hybrid role as teacher, adviser, and advocate that she calls "amazing."

Emma has yet to decide whether her professional role will be inside or outside the classroom; yet, she too discusses the need for a bridge between the two. Taking on formal and informal leadership roles in her school and district while remaining inside the classroom has allowed her to view teaching from both a macro- and micro-level. Emma's professional goal is "to be making a difference in the policies and programs" directly affecting her students. Her dream job "is making sure that kids are getting a really good education, to be way up high, making decisions about curriculum and policies at the school level." She recognizes, however, that completely leaving teaching to work solely at the district level would be unfulfilling and believes if she were to move out of the classroom to focus on curricular policy, she would need to find a way back in. "Somehow," she asserts, "I'd really need to teach a class! I love spending my days with kids." And though she's not sure what the job would look like that would allow her to influence students on a personal and political level, striking a balance between work in and out of the classroom is crucial.

Armando, too, believes a hybrid teacher-administrator role would best meet his personal and professional needs: effecting change on personal, schoolwide, and political levels. He describes his dream job as "teacher–activity director–principal":

> I think I would be happiest being a teacher and an activity director [and principal], you know? Yeah, I think a perfect job would involve being in a position like a principal to influence schoolwide policy, even if they're not always perceived in the most positive light, sometimes I think they're necessary. Yet at the same time having the

time to do a lot of the social activities I know are very important for a school, and yet at the same time be a teacher. So yeah, I guess the ideal job would be teacher–activity director–principal, if there were such a position.

Similarly, Diana is deeply committed to classroom teaching but attracted by the idea of making a broader impact. When asked if she would consider taking a job that would allow her to impact students and teachers, she responded enthusiastically to the notion of a hybrid teaching role:

> Oh, that would be glorious. I remember having some teachers who were in teaching, who were full-time teachers at elementary school in Santa Barbara, and then I guess they taught a couple of the graduate courses at night. . . . That would be wonderful, that would be so awesome for me as a professional. I would see students [and be able to say], "This is what I did this morning, and now here's what you can do." It would just be so instantaneous, right there.

Or, Diana might add, complementary. Such "dream" hybrid careers would allow professionals like the ones profiled here to have a direct impact on the lives of children while sharing their passion and expertise with others through mentoring, advocacy, or activism.

Increased job hybridity may mean that competent and committed individuals will be better able to construct meaningful careers that allow them to remain connected to the core work of teaching and learning while also working to change the system of schooling. We caution, however, that like all good reform ideas, job hybridity is a concept ripe for misuse. One need only witness the stressed-out "teacher-plus" ranks of young energetic educators who seek to do it all, but eventually must regroup, prioritize, and redefine the difference they seek to make. For some, this may feel like an erosion of idealism or a compromise. For others, it is an empowering opportunity to clarify their own hopes and dreams—carefully taking on a set of responsibilities within well-chosen contexts that they feel confident will help change the world through education.

DISCUSSION QUESTIONS

1. How can you create a "dream job" that gives you sufficient professional autonomy, embeds you in a variety of supportive social networks, and enables you to make a difference across many dimensions of the educational system—all while living a life that is happy and balanced?

2. What are some ways to simultaneously make a difference in education and still remain in close proximity to children? Which of these might interest you, and why? If this will require shifting out of full-time teaching at some point, how might you accomplish that?

3. If you are currently teaching, does your school or district provide support for reform-minded teachers who are seeking to make a difference both within and beyond their classroom? If not, how might you take action to create and support meaningful career pathways for educators?

4. If you are just entering the profession, what will you do to ensure that your first teaching position will support you to effect change both inside and outside the classroom?

FURTHER READING

Darling-Hammond, Linda, and Gary Sykes. 2009. *Teaching as the Learning Profession: Handbook of Policy and Practice*. San Francisco: Jossey-Bass.

Glickman, Carl D. 2004. *Letters to the Next President: What We Can Do About the Real Crisis in Public Education*. New York: Teachers College Press.

Lyons, K. B. "Preparing to Stay: An Examination of the Effects of Specialized Preparation on Urban Teacher Retention." Unpublished dissertation, University of California—Los Angeles.

Moore Johnson, Susan, and the Project on the Next Generation of Teachers. 2004. *Finders and Keepers: Helping New Teachers Survive and Thrive in Our Schools*. San Francisco: Jossey-Bass.

APPENDIX
UCLA's Longitudinal Study of Urban Educators

From 2000 to 2007 we participated in a research group (with Katherine Masyn, Andrew Thomas, and Joanna Goode) to study the careers of more than a thousand urban teachers prepared by Center X's experimental teacher education program. Using both quantitative and qualitative methods, we conducted a range of studies to answer the following questions:

1. What is the effect of specialized teacher preparation on retention?

2. What is the effect of career advancement on attrition among highly qualified urban educators?

3. What individual and school characteristics are associated with retention in high-poverty schools?

The results of our analyses are reported in the following written products. Quartz (in press) provides synthesis of these products.

Anderson, L., and B. Olsen. 2006. "Investigating Early Career Urban Teachers' Perspectives on and Experiences in Professional Development." *Journal of Teacher Education* (September/October): 359–377.

Goode, J., K. H. Quartz, K. B. Lyons, and A. Thomas. 2004. "Developing Teacher Leaders: Exploring the Multiple Roles of Beginning Urban Educators." *Journal of Teacher Education and Practice* 17(4): 417–431.

Lyons, K. B. 2007. "Preparing to Stay: An Examination of the Effects of Specialized Preparation on Urban Teacher Retention." Unpublished dissertation, University of California, Los Angeles.

Masyn, K., and K. H. Quartz. Under review. "Rethinking Our Priorities: Applying Advanced Methodology for Identifying Schools as Targets for Equity-Minded Policy."

Masyn, K., K. H. Quartz, and K. B. Lyons. Under review. "Why Do They Stay? Early Career Retention of Highly-Qualified Teachers in High-Poverty Urban Schools."

Olsen, B., and L. Anderson, 2007. "Courses of Action: A Qualitative Investigation in Urban Teacher Retention and Career Development." *Urban Education* 42(1): 5–29.

Quartz, K. H. In press. "The Careers of Urban Teachers: A Synthesis of Findings from UCLA's Longitudinal Study of Urban Educators." In M. Bayer and U. Brinkkjær, eds., *Anthology on Teachers' Career Trajectories*. New York: Springer.

Quartz, K. H., and TEP Research Group. 2003. "'Too Angry to Leave': Supporting New Teachers' Commitment to Transform Urban Schools." *Journal of Teacher Education* (March/April): 99–111.

Quartz, K. H., K. B. Lyons, and A. Thomas. 2005. "Retaining Teachers in High-Poverty Schools: A Policy Framework." In N. Bascia, A. Cumming, A. Datnow, K. Leithwood, and D. Livingstone, eds., *International Handbook of Educational Policy*. Dordrecht, Netherlands: Kluwer.

Quartz, K. H., A. Thomas, L. Anderson, K. Masyn, K. B. Lyons, and B. Olsen. 2008. "Careers in Motion: A Longitudinal Retention Study of Role Changing Patterns Among Urban Educators." *Teachers College Record* 110(6).

Thomas, A. 2005. "Social Networks and Career Paths of Urban Teachers: Effects of Career Decision-Related Communication Networks on Teacher Retention." Unpublished dissertation, University of California, Los Angeles.

———. 2007. "Career Orientation of Urban Educators: A Social Network Analysis of Teacher Attrition." *Theory and Practice in the Social Sciences* (3)1: 19–47.

REFERENCES

Apple, Michael. 1985. "Teaching and 'Women's Work': A Comparative Historical and Ideological Analysis." *Teachers College Record* 86(3): 455–473.

Argote, Linda. 1999. *Organizational Learning: Creating, Retaining, and Transferring Knowledge.* Norwell, MA: Kluwer Academic Publishers.

Ayers, William. 1995. *To Become a Teacher: Making a Difference in Children's Lives.* New York: Teachers College Press.

Bryk, Anthony S., and Barbara L. Schneider. 2002. *Trust in Schools: A Core Resource for Improvement.* New York: Russell Sage Foundation.

Clifford, Geraldine, and James Guthrie. 1988. *Ed School: A Brief for Professional Education.* Chicago: University of Chicago Press.

Cochran-Smith, Marilyn. 1998. "Teacher Development and Educational Reform." In Andy Hargreaves, Ann Lieberman, Michael Fullan, and David Hopkins, eds., *International Handbook of Educational Change.* Boston: Kluwer Academic Publishers, 916–951.

———. 2003. "The Multiple Meanings of Multicultural Teacher Education: A Conceptual Framework." *Teacher Education Quarterly* 30(2): 7–26.

———. 2000. "The Future of Teacher Education: Framing the Questions That Matter." *Teaching Education* 11(1): 13–23.

Cochran-Smith, Marilyn, and Susan Lytle. 1999. "Relationships of Knowledge and Practice: Teacher Learning in Communities." *Review of Research in Education* 24: 251–307.

———. 1993. *Inside/Outside: Teacher Research and Knowledge.* New York: Teachers College Press.

Darling-Hammond, Linda. 1997. *The Right to Learn: A Blueprint for Creating Schools That Work.* San Francisco: Jossey-Bass.

———. 2000. *Solving the Dilemmas of Teacher Supply, Demand, and Standards: How We Can Ensure a Competent, Caring, and Qualified Teacher for*

Every Child. New York: National Commission on Teaching and America's Future.

Darling-Hammond, L., and Bransford, J., eds. 2007. *Preparing Teachers for a Changing World: What Teachers Should Learn and Be Able to Do*. San Francisco: Jossey-Bass.

Darling-Hammond, Linda, and Gary Sykes. 2009. *Teaching as the Learning Profession: Handbook of Policy and Practice*. San Francisco: Jossey-Bass.

Engvall, Robert. 1997. *The Professionalism of Teaching*. Lanham, MD: University Press of America.

Fessler, Ralph, and Judith Christensen. 1992. *The Teacher Career Cycle: Understanding and Guiding the Professional Development of Teachers*. Boston: Allyn and Bacon.

Fosnot, Catherine, ed. 1996. *Constructivism*. New York: Teachers College Press.

Fullan, Michael, and Andrew Hargreaves. 1996. *What's Worth Fighting For in Your School*. New York: Teachers College Press.

Gay, Geneva. 2000. *Culturally Responsive Teaching: Theory, Practice, and Research*. New York: Teachers College Press.

Gittell, Ross, and Avis Vidal. 1998. *Community Organizing: Building Social Capital as a Development Strategy*. Thousand Oaks, CA: Sage Publications.

Gladwell, Malcolm. 2000. *The Tipping Point: How Little Things Can Make a Big Difference*. New York: Little, Brown, and Company.

Glickman, Carl D. 2004. *Letters to the Next President: What We Can Do About the Real Crisis in Public Education*. New York: Teachers College Press.

González, Norma, Luis C. Moll, and Cathy Amanti. 2005. *Funds of Knowledge: Theorizing Practices in Households, Communities, and Classrooms*. London: Routledge.

Hargreaves, Andy, and Michael Fullan. 2008. *Change Wars*. Bloomington, IN: Solution Tree.

Herbst, Jurgen. 1989. *And Sadly Teach: Teacher Education and Professionalization in American Culture*. Madison: University of Wisconsin Press.

Holmes Group Executive Board. 1986. *Tomorrow's Teachers: A Report of the Holmes Group*. East Lansing, MI: Holmes Group.

Huberman, Michael. 1989. "The Professional Life Cycle of Teachers." *Teachers College Record* 91(1): 31–57.

———. 1994. *The Lives of Teachers*. New York: Teachers College Press.

Hunt, Jean A. 1998. "Of Stories, Seeds, and the Promise of Social Justice." In W. Ayres, J. Hunt, and T. Quinn, eds., *Teaching for Social Justice: A Democracy and Education Reader*. New York: New Press.

Ingersoll, Richard. 2003. *Who Controls Teachers' Work: Power and Accountability in America's Schools*. Cambridge, MA: Harvard University Press.

Kohl, Herbert R. 1998. *The Discipline of Hope: Learning from a Lifetime of Teaching.* New York: The New Press.

Ladson-Billings, Gloria. 1995. "Toward a Theory of Culturally Relevant Pedagogy." *American Education Research Journal* 35: 465–491.

Lieberman, Ann, and Lynne Miller. 2001. *Teachers Caught in the Action: Professional Development That Matters.* New York: Teachers College Press.

Lortie, Dan C. 1975. *Schoolteacher: A Sociological Study.* Chicago: University of Chicago Press.

McPherson, Miller, Lynn Smith-Lovin, and James Cook. 2001. "Birds of a Feather: Homophily in Social Networks." *Annual Review of Sociology* 27: 415–444.

Meier, Deborah. 1995. *The Power of Their Ideas: Lessons for America from a Small School in Harlem.* Boston: Beacon Press.

Meier, Deborah, and George Wood. 2004. *Many Children Left Behind.* Boston: Beacon Press.

Milgram, Stanley. 1967. "The Small World Problem." *Psychology Today* 1(1): 60–67.

Moll, Luis. 1988. *Funds of Knowledge for Teaching: A New Approach in Education.* Keynote address, Illinois State Board of Education, February 5, 1998.

Moore Johnson, Susan, and the Project on the Next Generation of Teachers. 2004. *Finders and Keepers: Helping New Teachers Survive and Thrive in Our Schools.* San Francisco: Jossey-Bass.

Murphy, Marjorie. 1990. *Blackboard Unions: The AFT and the NEA, 1900–1980.* Ithaca, NY: Cornell University Press.

National Commission on Teaching and America's Future. 2003. *No Dream Denied: A Pledge to America's Children.* Washington, DC: National Commission on Teaching and America's Future.

National Partnership for Excellence and Accountability in Teaching. 2000. *Projects and Activities.* http://www/web3.educ.msu.edu/projects.html#recr.

Nieto, Sonia. 2003. *What Keeps Teachers Going?* New York: Teachers College Press.

Oakes, Jeannie. 1996. "Making the Rhetoric Real: UCLA's Struggle for Teacher Education That Is Multicultural and Social Reconstructionist." *Multicultural Education* 4: 4–10.

Oakes, Jeannie, and Martin Lipton. 2006. *Teaching to Change the World.* New York: McGraw-Hill.

Oakes, Jeannie, John Rogers, and Martin Lipton. 2006. *Learning Power: Organizing for Education and Justice.* New York: Teachers College Press.

Olsen, Brad, Sheila Lane, Eloise Metcalfe, Jody Priselac, Gordon Suzuki, and RaeJeane Williams. 2005. "Center X: Where Research and Practice Intersect for Urban School Professionals: A Portrait of the Teacher

Education Program at the University of California, Los Angeles." In Patrick Jenlink, ed., *Portraits of Teacher Preparation: Learning to Teach in a Changing America*. Lanham, MD: Scarecrow Education Press.

Piaget, Jean. 1954. *The Construction of Reality in the Child*. New York: Basic Books.

Rose, Mike. 1995. *Possible Lives: The Promise of Public Education in America*. New York: Penguin.

Samway, Katherine Davies, and Lucinda Pease-Alvarez. 2005. "Teachers' Perspectives on Open Court." In Bess Altwerger, ed., *Reading for Profit: The Commercialization of Reading Instruction*. Portsmouth, NH: Heinemann.

Sarason, Seymour. 1990. *The Predictable Failure of Educational Reform*. San Francisco: Jossey-Bass.

Shulman, Lee. 1986. "Those Who Understand: Knowledge Growth in Teaching." *Educational Researcher* 15(2): 4–14.

Sikes, Patricia, Linda Measor, and Peter Woods. 1985. *Teacher Careers: Crises and Continuities*. London: Falmer Press.

Stanton-Salazar, Ricardo. 2001. *Manufacturing Hope and Despair: The School and Kin Support Networks of Mexican Youth*. New York: Teachers College Press.

Tyack, David. 1974. *The One Best System: A History of American Urban Education*. Cambridge, MA: Harvard University Press.

Urbanski, Adam, and Carl O'Connell. 2003. *Transforming the Profession of Teaching: It Starts at the Beginning*. http://www.nctaf.org/article/?g=0&c=3&sc=13&ssc=0&a=39.

Weiner, Lois. 2005. *Urban Teaching: The Essentials*, rev. ed. New York: Teachers College Press.

Wenger, Etienne. 1998. *Communities of Practice: Learning, Meaning, and Identity*. New York: Cambridge University Press.

Yee, Silvia M. 1990. *Careers in the Classroom: When Teaching Is More Than a Job*. New York: Teachers College Press.

Zeichner, Kenneth. 1993. "Connecting Genuine Teacher Development to the Struggle for Social Justice." *Journal of Education for Teaching* 19: 5–20.

INDEX

accountability, 34, 124; structures, 128
action research, 32, 52, 119
activism, 89–90; social networks and, 130; within systems, 101, 135
Addams, Jane, 89
administration, 2; credentialing programs, 65, 77, 109; discipline and, 38; district, 21; influence of, 37–38; initiatives, 46; professional autonomy and, 37–38; relationships with, 67; salaries, 39; shifting to, 35–39
administrators: benefits of, 126; "the fight" and, 94; flexibility of, 118
adolescents, high-risk, 98
Advanced Placement courses, 91
advocacy, 39, 111, 125–126, 135
alumni networks, 67, 72–73, 82
assessments, 91, 113; alternative, 128; analysis of, 65; creativity and, 109; through relationships, 104–105; self, 48; standardized, 46; work in, 105. *See also* standardized testing

attorneys, 93
attrition, 22, 34, 36; school culture and, 69; in urban education, 3, 96
autonomy. *See* professional autonomy

balance, 51, 120–121; life-work, 51; multiple roles and, 75–80
Bay Area Math Project, 69, 71–72
Beginning Teacher Support and Assessment (BTSA), 47, 77
Big Picture schools, 78–79, 106
bilingualism, 40
bonding ties, 63, 82
bridging ties, 63, 71, 82
BTSA. *See* Beginning Teacher Support and Assessment
bureaucracy, 49; "the fight" and, 96; fighting, 91; urban education and, 32
bureaucratic centralization, 22
burnout, 113–114; avoiding, 80–81; professional autonomy and, 30; time and, 123
Burns, Marilyn, 103

teachers: career labels for, 88–89; categories, 15; of color, 35, 131; demographics of, 14, 131; development, 30, 34; education programs, 61; education staff v., 20–21; equity-minded, 84; hybrid roles for, 121; influence of, 37–38; intentions of, 15; lead, 120; as leaders, 21; perceptions of, 15; professional, 120; research, 52; resident, 120; salaries, 39; substitute, 46
teacher-scholars, 51–52
teacher support providers, 77
teaching: feminization of, 11; leaving, 109–110; maintaining connection to, 80–81; measures, 101; new vision of, 118–121; professionalizing, 11–12; quality, 103; respect for, 11; stages of, 120; traditions, 11–13; transformative, 118
territoriality, 68–69
testing: learning v., 41. *See also* standardized testing
time, 122–123; compatibility, 12; management, 80, 82
The Tipping Point (Gladwell), 62
Title I coordinators, 42–43
training, 29–31; leadership, 103
transience, 66

trust, 61, 69
turnover, 45–46

UCLA. *See* University of California at Los Angeles
uncertainty, 9–10, 121
University of California at Los Angeles (UCLA), 9, 12–15, 21, 40, 50, 69–70, 118; alumni networks and, 73; IDEA program, 51; social networks and, 76
urban education, 15–17, 131; attrition in, 3, 96; bureaucracy and, 32; burnout and, 113–114; commitment to, 44; hierarchical settings in, 34; social network types, 63–64; working conditions, 48–49
Urbanski, Adam, 120
U.S. National Center for Education Statistics Common Core Data, 21

vent sessions, 95

Waiver-to-Basic programs, 40
work ethic, 113
working conditions, 48–49
workshops, 126
The World Is Flat (Friedman), 102

Zeichner, Kenneth, 89–90

ABOUT THE AUTHORS

Karen Hunter Quartz is Director of Research at UCLA's Center X and is currently working on the design of a new school, UCLA Community School, in central Los Angeles.

Brad Olsen is Associate Professor of Education at the University of California–Santa Cruz. His research focuses primarily on teachers, teaching, and teacher education. Dr. Olsen previously worked as a high school English teacher, school administrator, and teacher educator. He is the author of *Teaching What They Learn, Learning What They Live: How Teachers' Personal Histories Shape Their Professional Development* (Paradigm Publishers 2008).

Lauren Anderson completed her Ph.D. in Urban Schooling at UCLA and is currently working as a postdoctoral fellow in the School of Education and Social Policy at Northwestern University.

Kimberly Barraza Lyons completed her Ph.D. in Urban Schooling at UCLA and is currently pursuing multiple roles as a researcher, university lecturer, school board president, and high school Spanish teacher.